Also by Doreen Tovey:

Cats in the Belfry
Cats in May
The New Boy
Donkey Work
Double Trouble
Life with Grandma
Raining Cats and Donkeys
Making the Horse Laugh
The Coming of Saska
A Comfort of Cats
Roses Round the Door
Waiting in the Wings

MORE CATS IN THE BELFRY

This edition published in 2009 by Summersdale Publishers Ltd.

First published by Bantam Press in 1995

Summersdale Publishers Ltd
46 West Street
Chichester
West Sussex
PO19 1RP
UK

www.summersdale.com

Printed and bound in Great Britain

ISBN: 978-1-84024-769-5

MORE
CATS
IN THE BELFRY

DOREEN TOVEY

summersdale

ONE

I could have bet on it. Within minutes of taking my new Siamese kitten, Shantung, into the garden for the first time, Mrs Binney was peering over the front gate, mouth turned down to match her hat-brim, gloomily predicting that I'd never raise her.

Mrs Binney, once as rare a sight in the valley as a cuckoo in December, had taken to haunting it since the death of my husband Charles the previous year. She'd told me several times that her son Bert fancied the cottage if I was thinking of selling. Whether she was keeping an eye on things from that angle – to see if I showed signs of moving – or whether she didn't want to miss the excitement if, in trying to maintain the place myself, I fell off a ladder, or out of a tree, or did myself a mischief with Charles's electric chainsaw, all of which she forecast constantly – the fact was that whenever I saw Mrs B. coming down the hill, my heart sank like a stone. It was like having Cassandra perpetually around in a po-shaped hat and ankle boots. It didn't help either that, where Shantung was concerned, I was inclined to agree with her.

Almost from the time we'd first had Siamese cats there'd been a blue-point queen and a seal-point male at the cottage. Our first Siamese had been a blue-point female called Sugieh, and when she'd had kittens one was a seal-point male with big feet and spotted whiskers whom we decided to keep as a companion for her and call Solomon (Solomon Seal, we thought, was rather good). When Sugieh herself died tragically when the kittens were three months old, we'd kept Sheba, her blue-point daughter, as company for Solomon, and the tradition had gone on from there.

For almost all that time, too, there'd been a donkey called Annabel bawling for peppermints over the half-door of her stable or keeping an eye on us from the hillside behind the cottage – small, wilful, her idea of a side-splitting joke being to butt us from behind when we weren't expecting it; loving us, for all that, as dearly as we loved her. She'd died three months after Charles, whom she'd adored, and Shebalu, Sheba's successor, had followed her within a year. The cottage and its big garden seemed so empty then, with only myself and Saska, the current seal-point boy, in it, that when I was unable to find a blue-point kitten quickly to restore that part of my life, at any rate, to normal I settled for a lilac-point instead.

There wasn't all that difference between blue- and lilac-points, I reasoned. They often occurred in the same litter. Just so long as there was a prissy little pale-coated girl around the place. Then I drove down to Devon to fetch her, met a twelve-week-old lilac-point for the first time, and wondered what I'd let myself in for. I'd never seen anything so fragile.

All Siamese kittens are white when they are born. Longer than ordinary kittens, blunt at both ends, they look exactly like those white Continental sausages, *boudins blancs*. When their colour points start to develop, however, while their bodies remain basically white, there are subtle variations in the whiteness. Seal-point kittens' bodies take on a creamish tinge; the bodies of blue-points have more of a milky hue; the two lilac-point kittens I was looking at were the purest ice-white, with the faintest shading on ears and paws like shadows on a snowfield and – I couldn't take my eyes off them – the oddest-coloured noses. A pronounced pinkish mauve as though they were Orphans of the Storm and not half feeling the cold.

Actually they were curled together in an armchair in front of a log fire in a huge old country sitting-room, with low-beamed ceilings, rugs on a polished oak floor and adult Siamese everywhere – draped over chairs, squatting on the bookcase, one on its back with its feet in the air in front of the big fire-basket in the inglenook, one coming in from the kitchen, another strolling out through the doorway into the hall...

Maybe it was the presence of so many big cats in full colour that made the kittens look so frail. One kitten, actually, at second glance. The other was bigger, more solid and confident-looking, regarding me with the calmest of periwinkle blue eyes. I would have picked her like a shot, but she was already spoken for. She was entered in a show for the following weekend and if she won a top award a breeder was going to have her. It was her sister who was for sale – the one who by comparison resembled a small white mouse and seemed just about as nervous. The moment she saw me looking at her she was flat on her stomach under the dresser, cringing away from me as if I were Sweeney Todd.

She was healthy, I knew. My friend Pauline Furber, a breeder herself, had found her for me. If Pauline said she was good, she was. It was just that she looked so fragile – as if rearing her would be like trying to raise a flower fairy. I thought of Saska and quailed. He was more like a miniature elephant. Rumbustious, clumsy-footed – supposing he stepped on her and squashed her? She looked so solemn, too. I wanted a lively kitten to cheer things up, not one apparently in training for a sainthood.

As if reading my thoughts, 'She's rather reserved,' said her breeder. 'We've never heard her purr yet – but she might be different if she weren't with all the other cats.' Maybe she would. That conclave of superior-looking felines was enough to intimidate anybody, sitting there, except for the one with its feet in the air, like a session of the House of Lords. 'She's got a beautiful head,' said Pauline, who'd come with me. She had indeed. She was a miniature Nefertiti in cat form, even if her sister did have the edge...

Hoping I was doing the right thing, I said I'd have her. It was May Day, a Sunday. I told her she was my small May Queen. It was also one of the worst May Days on record, cold and pouring with rain, hence the log fire at the breeder's. On the way back to Somerset we drove through a tremendous thunderstorm and the May Queen had diarrhoea in her basket. If she hadn't had a nervous stomach previously she certainly did from then on, what with the lightning, travelling in a car for the first time, and meeting up with Saska.

I'd carried her into the cottage in her basket and put it on the floor for his inspection, which was how we'd always introduced new kittens to older cats. The usual procedure was for the cat-in-residence to approach on its stomach, regard the kitten with horror through the wire door at the front of the basket, threaten to murder it if it didn't go away, then slink off, flat-eared, to sit on the sidelines and watch the effect. After a day or two of peering at it round corners and spitting if it came too close, the older one would capitulate, wash it all over to make it smell better (half the trouble in the first place was its having its mother's scent), and the next thing they'd be curled up together on the hearthrug or in a chair, the senior cat looking suitably sheepish at having given in. From then on it was Siamese United against the world.

Through the *front* of the basket was what mattered. That way the kitten could see its intimidator was another cat. Why Saska had to be different and spy through a gap in the wickerwork back goodness only knew, but Shantung had never seen a seal-point before – her world had consisted of blues and lilacs – and when she saw his black triangular face staring in at her through the little peephole she must have thought it was a cat-demon. She was very brave. Didn't make a sound. Just had diarrhoea again on the spot.

I did my best. Changed her blanket. Pulled the sofa across in front of the fire, put the basket on it, inserted a saucer of chicken and left the door ajar. In due course the sound of eating came from the depths. She didn't venture out, though. She stayed in hiding at the back, Saska sat on my lap in an adjacent armchair watching television, I worried like mad, and so we passed the evening.

I took her to bed with me that night in case she developed delayed shock. I hadn't a clue what to do if she did. I could hardly have given a kitten that size the kiss of life. But I put her, still in her travelling basket with a blanket and hotwater bottle in it, on the chest at the bottom of the bed and it was from there, once the light was out, that I heard her voice for the first time. She alternated between dozing for a few minutes and then waking up and screeching like a barn owl in the darkness for her mum. I switched on the lamp and brought her into bed with me. She scrambled out, hid in the basket, and yelled for her mum again. At half-past one, in desperation, I went down to fetch her some chicken, waking Sass as I passed his bed in front of the fire.

He came with me to the kitchen and started shouting for chicken himself. He could have been heard at the other end of the valley – probably was. He bawling downstairs, she wailing upstairs, half-past one in the morning and all the cottage lights on – it was like old times, I had to admit, even if it did occur to me that I needed my head read.

I gave him some, took a saucerful up to her. She wasn't backward in eating, that was one thing. The chicken vanished in a flash. She started to purr, which her breeder had said she didn't do. A purr so loud it filled the bedroom. I could hardly believe it. She rubbed her head against my hand. She was making the best of things, of course, as all kittens and puppies do. It is the innate law of survival – if Mum isn't around, tack on to whoever looks as if they might take care of you, the pointer being if they give you food.

For all that, the courage of such tiny creatures is astonishing. Humans would never be so philosophical. I got back into bed and this time she advanced up the eiderdown and crept into my arms like a small white snowflake. Overjoyed, I stroked her ears: upstanding lilac triangles reminiscent of a couple of pyramids on a miniature Egyptian skyline, that were the biggest thing about her. She liked me. Tomorrow would be a new beginning. It wouldn't take her any time to get used to Sass.

Like heck it wouldn't. I took the precaution of taking her basket downstairs ahead of her next morning and putting it on the sofa in case she needed a refuge, though I didn't think she would. I went into the hall and called her. I'd forgotten how steep the cottage stairs were for a kitten. She came down as if she was climbing Everest in reverse, front paws plopping down together, bottom perpendicular in the air. Nothing to that, she announced when she reached the bottom. Lay on, Macduff. Was it chicken again for breakfast?

Unfortunately Saska was crouched in ambush behind the sitting-room door and spat 'Tchaah' at her as she passed. She made for the sofa and into the basket as if shot from a gun and there she stayed for the rest of the day emerging only when he went out of the room, vanishing into the depths the moment he reappeared. When he was around, meals and litter box had to be handed in to her. She wasn't taking any chances. The evening passed like the previous one: Saska on my lap acting as if kittens had never been heard of – couldn't be one within *miles* – and boy, I gathered from his attitude, wasn't that Western good on the telly, look at those horses *run*; Shantung in the depths of the basket not making a sound; me with despondent visions of her living in there on the sofa for ever, and what sort of existence was that going to be for all of us?

Tuesday was much the same, except that was the day my school-teacher friends, Dora and Nita, came to see her, took her photograph with a Polaroid camera and said, as we watched it develop, that it was odd, but she didn't appear to be on it. She was, but you needed a magnifying glass to see her. For the occasion I'd got out the cats' Snoozabed, sent by an American reader years before as a present for Solomon and Sheba. It consisted of an enormous rectangle of foam rubber four inches deep, with an oval hollow big enough for several cats scooped out of its surface and a pale blue fur-fabric cover over the lot. 'Washable, hygienic, draught-proof – the ideal bed for your pets', read the wording on the outsize box in which it came, and the postman was so intrigued that he asked for days afterwards 'How'd they like the Snoozabed, then?' until in desperation I invited him in to see it, taking up most of the hearthrug with two cats stretched out in it like Turkish pashas, whereupon he said 'Trust the Yanks to think up something like that' and went off, as was duly reported back to me, to tell everybody else on his rounds that I had friends over in America as daft as I was.

Successive generations of Siamese had luxuriated in it; since Shebalu's death Saska had slept alone in it at night; and now, as he was out in his garden run, I draped a pale pink blanket over it as she was a girl and put Shantung in it to have her photo taken.

What with her hiding in the folds of the blanket from the two strangers she was sure had come to kidnap her, and the fact that film colour can vary, the picture that came out was what appeared to be an expanse of pale pink sand-dunes with, if one looked hard enough, a couple of pallid pyramids faintly visible over the top of one of them. 'Shantung's ears,' I said, pointing them out. Nita told me later that that was the moment *she* decided I'd never raise her, but she hadn't liked to say so.

Wednesday morning was when Mrs Binney gave me her opinion, overheard as he came up the lane by my neighbour Father Adams, who called out to me to take no notice of she, she'd put the damper on th' Angel Gabriel hisself if he listened to her, to which Mrs B. replied that he was a daft old fool and marched up the hill in high dudgeon. Wednesday I spent reflecting on how right Mrs Binney probably was – about Shantung, at any rate. And on Wednesday evening something happened.

I was sitting in an armchair sewing. Saska lay curled in the opposite one, his black whip tail over his nose. Between us, on the sofa, was the cat basket – from which, after a while, there stealthily emerged the small white figure of the May Queen. She paused, studying the recumbent form across the way. The Big Cat was obviously asleep. Paw by paw she crept along the sofa on to the armchair and crouched there, studying him intently. At that point he snored a resounding snore, woke up with a start, saw her looking at him practically nose to nose, and nearly hit the ceiling, after which he hid under the bookcase while the May Queen fled for her basket.

Next day, presumably having taken comfort from the fact that he hadn't eaten her so far, she ventured into the Snoozabed while he was in the garden house and stayed there when I brought him in. He made no attempt to frighten her, but sat on a nearby chair looking long-suffering. By Thursday evening they were walking past each other across the room – obviously deliberately, and obviously equally deliberately ignoring each other. And on Friday evening, washing up after supper, with the door to the sitting-room open so that I could rush to her rescue if need be, as they still showed no real sign of becoming friendly, I nearly dropped a plate with astonishment when something big and dark flashed past the open doorway closely followed by something small and white travelling like a midget express train.

Before I could move, they hurtled back in the opposite direction, Shantung whizzing along in front this time, ears flattened for lessened wind resistance, Saska bounding behind her in full chase. I peered furtively round the corner after them. Shantung, all six inches of her, had stopped and was sitting in the middle of the floor with a paw raised, daring Saska, advancing across the carpet on his stomach, to come One Step Nearer and she'd Bop Him – and Saska, everything forgotten save that he had a girl to play with again, was looking happier than he'd done in weeks.

One small hiccup barred the progress of the entente cordiale. Later that evening, ensconced in his favourite armchair with Shantung between his front paws, washing her fit to flatten her to show she was now one of the family, Saska slipped his tongue accidentally into one of her ears. The rest of her, having been around the place for nearly a week, had obviously acquired the cottage smell by this time and was acceptable. Protected by those enormous pyramids, however, the insides of her ears still bore the taint of other cats and places. He withdrew his tongue, curled back his lips in the familiar feline gesture of having just smelled something unbelievably awful, and said 'Tchaah' again – which could have set things right back to square one but for the fact that Shantung took no notice, presumably having decided that he was a bit potty and did that sort of thing from time to time, or else that it was me he was swearing at. As she didn't respond to his Monster act he considered the situation for a moment, steeled himself, then shut his eyes and licked the inside of both ears thoroughly until they tasted right. Had to be done Some Time, he said – after which they curled together in a white and seal-coloured ball and went to sleep. Things at the cottage were apparently back to normal.

TWO

Not quite, they weren't. Saska, having been looked after for as long as he could remember first by his mother and then by Shebalu, obviously thought that was what female cats were for, and was anxious to re-establish the fact as soon as possible – to which end, having been accustomed to stretching out in the Snoozabed using Shebalu as a pillow, within no time I found him trying to do it with Shantung. She was so small he looked quite ridiculous, spread there like a big brown ink blot with only her tiny head poking out from underneath him. Time and again I rushed to rescue her only to find her purring like a barrel organ, obviously revelling in what she thought was his fond attention. I hoped she wouldn't complain if one day she came out flat, I told her.

The business of his washing her didn't last long, either. Within days she was washing him, and he was expecting it. It was a mammoth task. He used to sit upright for it and it looked as if she'd taken on cleaning the Post Office tower, but it didn't daunt her. As fragile looking as the delicate Oriental silk after which she was named, she reached up to lick his ears as if they were the stars on the twin pinnacles of her ambition – as they probably were. She had a Big Cat to herself. She was Important. Life was Blissful, she kept on telling me.

It was a complete transformation from the timid little scrap I'd first seen in Devon – as if she'd been kept under by the other cats she'd lived with and was now making up for lost time. She consistently climbed things, fell off them, ate things she shouldn't and told the world about it in the loudest voice I'd ever heard in a kitten. She even talked in her sleep. One of my most vivid memories of her kittenhood is of the two of them curled together in front of the fire in the Snoozabed – Shantung muttering dozily away with her eyes shut, Saska regarding her exasperatedly with one eye open. Shebalu never did that, said his expression.

It was during this period that she developed a quirk she retains to this day. She objects to my using a typewriter. I only have to get it out and set it on the small table by the fire and even before I begin tapping on it she will, without opening her eyes, start protesting in a staccato, Morse code-like voice at my doing Any Such Thing while she, with her Sensitive Hearing, is in the room. I am used to it now. I take no notice and eventually the nattering, not unlike the tapping of typewriter keys itself, subsides – but it was pretty off-putting when she started it as a shrimp-sized kitten. None of our long line of cats had ever done that before, either.

Out of doors presented more problems. Situated as the cottage is, in a valley surrounded by pine-clad hills, with the metalled lane ending at the front gate and other than that only rough bridlepaths for horse-riders and a few neighbours' cars to bump over, we used to consider it the safest of places for animals to live in. Then Seeley, Solomon's successor, went out one Sunday morning when he was six years old and was never seen again. He couldn't have been run over – we and our neighbours searched for days and we'd have found his body if he had been. Either somebody stole him or – for like all Siamese he was extremely inquisitive – he must have got into a parked car at the top of the hill or along at the pub and been carried off accidentally. If so, we only hoped, since nobody brought him back in answer to our advertising, that whoever found him looked after him and grew to love him as we had done. But after that we decided that never again would any of our cats be allowed to run free unless we were with them. To lose any animal is heartbreaking, and where Siamese are concerned, with their striking appearance and obvious value, the temptation to people without conscience is no doubt considerable. So we trained Shebalu and Seeley's successor, Saska, to collars and leads; they wore them when Charles exercised them in the morning while I was getting breakfast, or when we took them for walks in the forest; and we put up a chalet and large wire run in the garden in which, when the weather was good, they sunned themselves when we weren't on hand to keep an eye on them. After Shantung came I used to take Saska out for his walk and garden inspection on his lead, then put him in the run and keep Tani, as I soon started calling her, with me while I did the household chores, with occasional sorties on the lawn for kitten exercise where Mrs Binney usually caught up with us and delivered her dismal predictions. Then, when I thought they were sufficiently used to each other for Sass not to pounce on Tani in mistake for a fieldmouse, I started to take them into the garden together.

It would have been impossible to get a collar small enough for Tani, so as in my experience none of our cats, as kittens, had ever strayed far from whoever was with them, I let her and Saska go loose – keeping close behind him so that I could grab him if he tried to make off. He didn't. Indoors, playing with Tani where only I could see him, was one thing. Outdoors he had his Siamese image to think of. So he pretended he didn't know her, stalking across the lawn or along the paths with aloof dignity while she pranced beside him like a furry yoyo trying to get his attention, or – a game she invented for herself as her legs grew longer – rushing up behind him as he walked and leap-frogging clean over him from back to front, which caused him only to swerve and stalk straight on, a look of resignation on his face, while she ran after him, gathering herself for the next leap.

Mrs Binney, watching with raised eyebrows, opined that she'd got St Vitus's Dance – a diagnosis which, as I was pretty sure that cats didn't get it, for once didn't worry me. Father Adams, who had once owned a Siamese himself – Mimi, who'd been given to him when her owner went abroad and whom he'd worshipped till the day she died – said nostalgically that he 'ouldn't mind a little 'un like that himself: minded him of his girl, she did. And Fred Ferry, our reputed local poacher who'd been interested in Siamese potential ever since he'd watched Saska, as a youngster, retrieving fir cones and fallen apples when I threw them and bringing them back to me, said he bet if she was trained she'd be a good rabbit catcher when she got older.

Mrs Binney, continuing her efforts on behalf of her son Bert, meanwhile took the opportunity to lean on the gate one day, remark how thin she thought Shantung was looking, and enquire in a lowered voice whether I knew that Mr Myburn had been complaining about 'they trees up thur'? The Myburns owned a bungalow whose garden and adjoining portion of field abutted on the top of the cottage orchard, and the four trees in question, which were in the orchard hedge, overhung a wooden shed on their property. One of my many maintenance worries had been whether the trees, which were old and gnarled, could possibly come down in a storm and cause damage for which I might be held liable – from which point my imagination carried me on to see myself faced with a large claim which I would be unable to pay. Mr Myburn would undoubtedly be in the line of fire when the shed collapsed, I'd have to sell the cottage, and the cats and I would end up living in a garret... all the things people like me are apt to imagine when so much as a roof tile comes off. The obvious solution was to have the trees taken down by an expert but I knew I couldn't afford that, so I'd done nothing, gone on worrying, and here was Mrs Binney playing on my fears.

Who had Mr Myburn complained to? I asked. 'Everybody,' said Mrs B. encouragingly. 'If they belonged to my Bert he'd take 'em down hisself,' she added, patently confident that if I could be persuaded into selling the cottage the orchard would automatically go with it. 'He says they could fall down any time.'

Glancing upwards to make sure they hadn't done it yet, I made my excuses, picked up Tani, withdrew into the cottage to worry some more, and that evening marched up to see Mr Myburn. I'd heard he was concerned about the trees in the orchard hedge, I told him. He said he was. Well, I volunteered, I couldn't afford to pay for them to be cut down professionally, but I was pretty adept with Charles's electric chainsaw, and if he would help me I thought I could take them down myself. How about it?

Help? he enquired, obviously not seeing himself as a woodsman. If I cut them straight down they certainly would come down on his shed, I explained. They needed to be sawn part way through, then pulled sideways with a rope so that they fell into his field. If he would just help with the rope after I'd tied it on... He could have the wood if he liked, I added. I couldn't possibly drag the trees back down to the cottage...

Brightening visibly at the prospect of a supply of winter logs Mr Myburn agreed, and the following Saturday morning saw me lugging an extending ladder up the steep hillside opposite the cottage to the orchard hedge; carting the chainsaw, its long cable and a can of chain oil up the same way; and bidding a soulful farewell to Tani and Saska, locked in their run with a notice on the door telling whoever it might concern whom to contact if I didn't come back – which, donning my riding hat and rubber boots and gloves (helpful, I understood, if one cut through the cable by mistake), I privately considered a strong possibility.

I thought Mrs Myburn might provide a cup of coffee before we started, but no. Mr Myburn stood ready wearing his rubber boots and a yellow construction worker's safety helmet which he'd presumably borrowed, Mrs Myburn peered apprehensively from the shelter of the bungalow doorway, and work was obviously expected to start right away.

With Mr Myburn's help I threaded the ladder from the top of the bank up through the intricacies of the first tree, climbed it, tied the top of it to a hefty branch for safety, fetched up the saw, primed the oil button and began cutting. Most of the branches dropped neatly into the field or over the hedge on the orchard slope. It was when I secured a long rope to a branch that overhung the shed, cut partly through it, got down and asked Mr Myburn to help me pull it sideways that Mrs Myburn sprang into action. 'No, darling! No!' she shrieked, rushing forward as if I'd suggested he jump off the Matterhorn. 'You mustn't! It's dangerous!'

When I pointed out that with two of us pulling on a thirty-foot rope, both feet on the ground and standing way beyond the range of the length of the branch, it was perfectly safe, but that I couldn't pull it on my own and if I cut right through the branch instead and just let it drop it *would* land on the shed, she capitulated. Hands clasped in prayer, she stood by as we pulled the branch sideways and Mr Myburn held it there while I shinned up the ladder and severed it completely. 'Oh, Leslie, you are brave,' she cooed while I climbed down and prepared to move the ladder.

We got all four trees down like that – first the branches, then the trunks – until a large pile of timber lay on the ground in the Myburns' field and their shed was out of danger. I hadn't the strength to cut the wood into logs for them, and I wasn't lending Mr Myburn my saw. One thing you have to do with an electric saw – which he didn't know, never having used one – is to press the oil button at very frequent intervals, otherwise the chain will dry out and the motor overheat. He'd questioned my pumping it as often as I did – they didn't do that with petrol ones, he said, his tone conveying that, as a woman, I didn't understand these things. Maybe not, but engine-powered saws work on a different oiling system, and I had no intention of having my electric one ruined. It was essential for the cottage wood supply for the winter. So I made the excuse that I had work to do with it later, trailed back down to the cottage with the equipment, took the notice off the cat-run door, telling them 'I'm back, chaps. We're all right for a while yet – I *did* it', and tottered indoors to have some bread and cheese before collapsing into an armchair. All afternoon I could hear Mr Myburn up at the top of the hill, industriously cutting logs with a saw borrowed elsewhere. Every now and then it stopped and, from the stuttering noises, proved difficult to start again. I hoped he understood the mechanism of that one.

One thing it did bring home to me was that as a widow I was indeed a social outcast as far as some people were concerned. Immediately after Charles's death many people had called offering sympathy, going out of their way to be friendly. 'It doesn't last,' I was told by other women who'd gone through the experience before me. 'People don't really want you when you're on your own. They soon start to drop you.'

How true that had turned out to be. In the old days, if Charles and I had been taking down those trees together, we'd have been asked in for coffee before we started. It would have been a friendly get-together. Now I was fended off as if I had the plague, or might expect further help with something.

The Myburns weren't the only ones, either. One couple, Rhona and Paul, with whom Charles and I had been very friendly – we played cards together regularly – actually told me, when we met by accident some weeks after his death, that they'd seen me one day in the supermarket in Cheddar but had kept out of my way. 'We thought you wouldn't want to talk to anybody,' they said.

What they meant was that they hadn't wanted to talk to *me*, and were only telling me now in case I'd happened to see them. The only time we met again after that was when Rhona's mother, herself a widow, came to stay with them. I was invited over to tea, and to go and see a place they were thinking of buying. It seemed they had the idea of starting up a boarding cattery and kennels and had found an old house with large grounds and an attached barn that could, they said, be turned into a granny flat. Several granny flats from the size of it. If they could get planning permission Rhona's mother, parked docilely side by side in the back of their car with me as if we were already in our wheelchairs, was going to sell her own house in Essex, put the money towards the capital they needed, and have a flat with them. Did they hope I might consider doing the same? I wondered. I preserved an unimpressed silence, countered Paul's remark as I left that evening that the car I was driving – bought six weeks before Charles's sudden death – was too big for me with the reply that I needed it to pull our caravan, which I intended to go on using, and never heard from them again.

There was likewise a man who lived at the other end of the village but was grazing some goats in a field further past the cottage. He always used to stop and chat to Charles, but after his death would pass by, when I was in the garden, looking straight ahead and pretending not to see me – until the day when, after a tremendous gale during the night, I was standing on top of one of the big flat cottage gateposts, chainsaw in hand, preparing to deal with a branch of the damson tree that had split off from the main bough and was hanging like a vast, leafy curtain across the front gate.

The goat man, trudging past on his usual morning visit, stopped and looked across at me. Oh good, I thought. He was going to offer to hold the branch while I sawed. Like heck he was. Would I be going out that afternoon? he asked, and when I said I wouldn't he said he and his wife would be away for the rest of the day and one of the goats was due to kid. Would I keep an eye on her and phone the vet if necessary? I said that I would and he went on his way, apparently without noticing that I was arched on the gatepost like Nelson on his column, preparing to saw off an awkward branch, and might have appreciated assistance.

That was why I put up with Mrs Binney's visits as patiently as I did instead of, as Father Adams and Fred Ferry continually advised me, 'giving she a kick in the pants'. They meant it, metaphorically, of course. Father Adams, who'd been at school with her, always referred to her as Old Mod (her name was Maude). Old Mod, he said, had been a misery for as long as he could remember. She was a widow too, though. Always referring to the fact. Always talking to me of 'people in our position' or 'people of our age' – which at times made me feel like taking Father Adams's advice since she was, I knew, a good twenty years older than I was.

But she was obviously lonely. Probably felt as bereft of people who cared about her as I did at times – which was why my mouth fell open and stayed that way when she told me one day that there was somebody in the village who was keen on her.

'Spicy bit of news then?' enquired Father Adams, happening to pass by as usual at the crucial moment.

'Oh... no...' I managed to get out, while Mrs Binney gave him a look that should have withered him on the spot. It wasn't just spicy, it was electrifying. The revelation that Mrs B., of all people, had an admirer.

THREE

That was her interpretation of events, at any rate. There was, with its headquarters over in the centre of the village so that living a mile and a half away in the valley I knew little of its goings-on except by hearsay, a Friendly Hands Social Club which catered mostly for the over-sixties but, in order to augment its numbers, welcomed widows and widowers of any age. I'd been invited to join it myself after Charles died, but I felt that life held more for me yet than the excitement of a monthly communal visit by a chiropodist from the local health centre, or annual holidays by coach to Aberdeen or Durham, where the party stayed in the unoccupied university hall of residence during the students' vacation and was shepherded on daily sightseeing tours by the enthusiastic element that inevitably emerges as leaders of such organisations, and so I made my excuses. I was fully occupied with the cottage, the cats and writing. I took my van away on holidays. I didn't go out in the evenings if I could help it – not winter evenings, anyway, since in turning in to the cottage driveway in the dark I could easily land myself and the car in the stream.

Not so Mrs Binney, who went to anything that offered tea, biscuits and the chance of a gossip, especially when it was held in the village hall, a matter of yards down the road from her house. She'd been sitting non-participantly in the front row of what Fred Ferry called the Old Trouts' Knees-up for years until fate suddenly took a hand by arranging the demise of the octogenarian who'd hitherto played the piano for the Singalong Half-hour that wound up every meeting. When nobody else volunteered for the job, Mrs Binney unexpectedly upped and offered her services as accompanist – and, to everybody's surprise, did it very well. Father Adams's wife, who belonged to the club herself and kept me up to date with what went on there, said she didn't remember Maude Binney learning the piano as a girl – maybe she'd done it while she was away in service – but she could play all right. 'Sally', 'Keep Right On to the End of the Road', 'Silver Threads among the Gold'...

'Ah,' I said, recollecting the evening back in the spring when I'd passed the village hall on foot on my way home from a meeting of the History Society at the chairman's house, where we were planning the reissue of the village history we'd done a few years before, and I'd heard 'Sally' being belted out with such vigour it sounded as if the piano was coming through the corrugated tin roof at any moment. That explained it. I liked to know these things. I'd wondered at the time who was making all that noise.

Anyway, it seemed that the Singalong leader was a Mr Tooting who, with his wife, had retired to the village from the Midlands some years earlier. His wife had since died and Mr Tooting, distinguishable at any distance around the village by the fact that he was short, wore glasses, a military moustache, an air of supreme self-importance and a checked tweed pork-pie hat, had thereafter thrown himself into helping run local affairs. He was the most active churchwarden the Rector had ever had, always ready to organise beating the bounds, head a sub-committee for repairs to the organ, or personally oversee the men re-leading the roof. He fetched the old people's medicines en bloc from the chemist in the next village if they left their prescriptions in a special box in the post office, and was secretary of the Gardening Club, the Boys' Club and the Friendly Hands Club, at which he conducted the Singalong Half-hour by standing beside the piano, waving his arms at the audience as if trying to levitate them out of their seats, and leading the songs in a hearty baritone.

According to Mrs Adams, on the occasion of Mrs Binney's acting as accompanist for the first time, he bowed to her afterwards, led her forward by her fingertips as if they were dancing a minuet, and presented her to the audience, who supposed they must be meant to clap and obligingly did so. 'And then,' said Mrs A. with meaning, 'he kissed 'er 'and.' I could just imagine it. Mr Tooting doing a pint-sized impression of the conductor of the London Philharmonic at the last night of the Proms.

What did Mrs Binney do?' I enquired.

'Turned red as a beetroot and showed her teeth,' said Mrs Adams.

I could imagine that, too. Mrs Binney's smile, fortunately rare, was the result of somewhat antiquated dentistry and reminded most people of a horse about to bite.

Mr Tooting, still busy bowing to the audience, must have missed that bit. From then on all the Singalong Half-hours ended with his leading Mrs B. forward for applause, escorting her to her chair in the front row while he returned to the platform to read out the notices, and afterwards helping her on with her coat and walking with her to her front door, which was only a few yards up the lane, on his own way home, and anyway he had a torch. It didn't fail to arouse comment in the village, however.

'Tryin' to hang her hat up there all right.'

'Fancies herself livin' in thic bungalow.' 'Flatten he like a steam-roller on thur weddin' night', was Fred Ferry's country-candid observation to me outside the post office one day as we watched them walking up the village street together.

They were walking up the street together – big, brawny Mrs Binney and bantam-sized Mr Tooting – because she'd spotted him from behind her curtains as he passed her gate and had nipped out to catch him up. Mrs Tucker, who lived opposite her and kept a watchful eye on village goings-on from behind her own curtains, said she was always doing that.

Given that she'd decided he was interested in her, Mrs Binney was obviously doing her best to further matters – to which end, rocking the village to its stolid foundations, and as suddenly as she'd volunteered to play the piano, one day she abandoned the chamber-pot hat and drainpipe coat she'd worn ever since I could remember and appeared, first of all in the post office and later the same day in the valley, wearing a Picasso-patterned summer dress and a hairdo of violet bubble-curls.

Father Adams was talking to me at the cottage gate when she came somewhat self-consciously down the hill. 'Gawd, Mod,' he said, stopping in mid-sentence to stare at her in feigned astonishment. 'Thee'st look like a hyacinth wrapped up in a Tesco bag. What on earth'st thee bin doin' to theeself?'

Ignoring him, she patted her curls complacently and asked me how I liked it. 'I... er... hardly recognised you,' I stammered, which was obviously the right answer because, while Father Adams faded quietly into the background and disappeared – no doubt to tip his cronies at the top of the hill not to miss on her way back – she confided to me that Shirl had done it. Took all last night, she had, doin' the perm. *And* made the dress for her. Very handy with her sewing machine, was Shirl. Appreciating the effort needed to construct a dress that fitted Mrs B.'s large and angular form in any material, let alone matching up sections of white nylon patterned with red, yellow and green triangles, I said she certainly must be.

Shirl, I would explain, was Mrs Binney's son Bert's girl-friend. Twenty years back she would have been living with her parents in the nearby seaside town where she was a hairdresser, with Bert zooming over on his motor-bike to court her in the evenings and at weekends.

In these days of couples no sooner fancying each other than moving in together, however, Shirl and Bert were ensconced in a caravan behind the Barage on the main road where Bert worked as a mechanic, while they looked around for something permanent.

Twenty years back Mrs Binney would have disowned Bert and written off Shirl as a brazen hussy, if not a daughter of Jezebel, but as they were only emulating what went on on the telly, and even, if rumour was to be believed, in some of the yuppy-owned big houses around the district, what, Mrs B. demanded of her neighbours, not without a touch of pride in her Bert's being among the avant-garde, could she do about it?

It was none of my business. Indeed, what with the dress, the violet hairdo and the piano-playing I began to wonder about her own intentions towards Mr Tooting. Did she see herself as Thoroughly Modern Maude, sharing his bungalow as Shirl shared the caravan with Bert? And if so, with her being a member of the Mothers' Union and Mr Tooting a churchwarden, what would the Rector say?

For the moment, at any rate, it made my life considerably easier. She gave up coming down the hill quite so often to bemoan the condition of the cottage garden or tell me that I'd never raise Tani – and Tani, almost magically, started to thrive.

She still had nervous diarrhoea at the drop of a hat but Pauline's vet, whose practice was twenty-five miles away from me but worth the journey because he had Siamese cats himself and understood them, prescribed charcoal and kaolin granules to mix with her food.

That controlled the diarrhoea and she started to put on weight.

She started to stand up to Saska, too. When he was indoors, where he didn't have to keep up his public image of an Eminently Superior Prince from Siam, he had a habit of trying to frighten her, when he thought I wasn't watching, by lowering his head, flattening his ears and stalking round her in a menacing circle while she crouched at bay on the carpet. Then one day I saw her, instead of crouching, lying on her side with one long back leg extended stiffly against him, fending him off like somebody using a boat-hook, and one front paw outstretched ready to hit him. As he moved round her she revolved correspondingly, as if on a pivot, so that she was always facing him, and when he couldn't find a point from which to pounce on her he gave up and pretended he was just passing by en route for food.

That was another thing. Fortified by the charcoal and kaolin she began to bolt her own meals and then start eating his, and I had to feed them separately so that he got his share undisturbed. So it was that one morning I came down, gave Saska his breakfast in the sitting-room and Tani hers in the kitchen, nipped out into the yard to change their litter trays, pulling the back door, which had a Yale lock, behind me to stop her following me – all part of a Siamese cat-owner's routine – and realised, even as I slammed it, that I'd locked myself out.

Normally I kept a spare key in the woodshed, but the previous day I'd gone out in the car, tossed my handbag on to the back seat after shopping and found, when I got home, that its contents had fallen out on the car floor. I'd gathered them up, put the car away and come down to the cottage to discover that the back door key wasn't in its usual place in my handbag. I thought it must be still on the floor of the car, decided to leave it until next day, and used the spare key from the woodshed instead.

That was the one now marooned indoors on the kitchen dresser – along with the car keys, so that I couldn't go up and look for the original door key on the car floor either.

Panicking about what the cats might do if left where they were – they normally expected to go out into the garden directly after breakfast – I fetched a ladder and a screwdriver, climbed on to the sloping hall roof, thankful that for once nobody was about to ask what I was doing, and crawled up it to the spare room window. Joy oh joy! As I thought! I'd left the casement slightly ajar for air when I'd cleaned it a few days previously. I raised the catch with the screwdriver, climbed in and belted downstairs – passing a puzzled Saska who had just finished his breakfast and couldn't make out why I'd come in through that door when I'd gone out through the other one, and a claustrophobic Tani who'd been marooned in the kitchen without anybody for company and didn't like it – shot out into the yard to fetch the litter trays which I knew they must by now be in urgent need of – and realised immediately that I'd done it again. Slammed the door behind me without thinking and locked myself out.

There was no point in trying the spare room window this time. I'd fastened the latch properly when I got in. I moved the ladder and tried the boxroom window over the kitchen. No go. Charles had long ago secured that one against intruders and I had kept it like that, with wire wound round the latch and bar. I climbed down and called to Tani through the back door keyhole to be a good girl. I wouldn't be long getting back to her, I said. I'd Better Not Be, she screeched back with the promise of imminent stomach upset in her voice. Where was Saska? Where was her BOX? she demanded in a rising soprano.

I rushed round to the sitting-room window and instructed Saska likewise. Where was Tani? Was I taking her out Without Him? he bawled, standing on the window sill with his tail raised threateningly against the curtain.

'Oh no!' I wailed aloud. 'Don't let him do that!' Saska had an unfortunate habit of spraying when he was upset about anything. I hadn't any idea whom I was asking. I didn't suppose the Almighty would be greatly concerned at my being locked out of the cottage through my own stupidity or the prospect of Saska spraying up the curtains. I often asked Charles for help when I couldn't find things or was in a predicament and it was surprising – sometimes to the point of being uncanny – how often the situation resolved itself. But I couldn't expect Charles to help me over this. And judging by Saska's tail the matter was urgent.

I ran down the lane to the Reasons'. Father Adams wasn't on the phone. Janet Reason had already gone off to her job at the nearby airport. Peter was just getting ready to leave himself. Could I use their phone to ring the police? I asked, explaining what had happened. When I rang the local police station, however, an answering machine informed me that it wasn't manned, and I should dial 999 if there was an emergency.

It was an emergency as far as I was concerned, I told the voice that answered when I did, explaining that if someone could come and open the car for me I could get the key of the cottage. I was given the number of Taunton police station, where they said they only had a few car keys. I'd better try the AA; they'd give me the number. There a female voice said I'd got their Travel Bureau, which didn't open until nine o'clock. What did I want? I told her, including the urgency about the cats' litter boxes. She was most sympathetic. Wouldn't they hold on? she asked, passing me swiftly to Emergency, who said someone would be me within an hour.

An hour! I tottered back up the lane, imagining the mayhem Tani might commit in the kitchen, and Saska against the sitting-room curtains, in that time. When Peter drove past a few minutes later, leaning out of his car window to ask was I all right, because I'd told him I was going back to wait for the AA, I was once more up on the hall roof, tapping away hammer and screwdriver.

'Fine,' I answered, more brightly than I felt. 'Had a sudden idea. Almost in. Any minute now.' It was something I'd seen Charles do on odd occasions when we'd been locked out – and sure enough, even as I spoke somehow I'd tapped the window frame enough for me to jolt the catch loose, insert the screwdriver, lift it up... and I was in again, downstairs, giving the cats clean litter boxes. In the Nick of Time, Tani announced, jumping into hers with evident relief, while I put the key in the outside lock so it couldn't happen again.

Now I just had to ring the AA and say there was no need for them to come. In my agitation I couldn't find their number in the phone directory. I decided to open the car now that the car keys were available, get the number from the AA book, which was in the door pocket, and retrieve the other back door key that had been the cause of all the trouble. I couldn't believe it when I couldn't find the key on the car floor. I phoned the AA, turned out my handbag once more in desperation and there, after all the panic, it was. Hidden in a corner, where it must have been all the time.

The next silly thing I did was get in a muddle over Tani's spaying. She should have the operation at six months, the vet had told me when he treated her for her nervous stomach. She'd been born at the end of January... six months from January was June, I calculated. I booked her in for the end of June and had driven her almost the twenty-five miles to the vet's on the appointed day when it dawned on me that six months from January was July. Tani was only five months old.

I drove on to the surgery to explain. Some cats were big enough earlier, said the vet, examining her. But definitely not Tani. She was still very small – needed to grow a bit more. She was a lovely little girl all the same, he said, cuddling her closely, which she decided was what she'd come for. So I brought her home for another month, unwisely told Miss Wellington what had happened, and started her off on another of her campaigns – which this time was not to have Tani spayed at all, but to let her have kittens.

Miss Wellington will be remembered by my readers as the elderly lady who concerned herself deeply with everything that happened in our part of the village.

Whenever the stream flooded in the valley, though her own cottage was at the top of the hill and she was in no way inconvenienced by it, she took it on herself to patrol the swallet – the large natural hole in the limestone bed of the stream higher up in the forest down which the surplus water was supposed to go but very often didn't. She rang the Council to tell them when it was blocked with silt – and again when they didn't arrive at the double to unblock it. She foresaw catastrophe every time it snowed, rained hard or the wind got up to gale force, and scurried round trying to organise forces to counter whatever threatened – masculine forces if possible, so that the male residents of the valley usually took cover when they saw her coming, though she did once suggest that she and I should move an enormous tree trunk to stop the overflow from the swallet sweeping down the bridlepath. In vain I protested that I would do myself an injury. Before I knew it I was on the other end of the log, struggling like Samson to shift it.

Way back when Annabel was young Miss Wellington had tried hard to persuade us to let her have a foal. Every time she went to stay with her friend who lived by the sea in Devon she would send us postcards showing mother donkeys on the beach with their cuddlesome offspring and *Some day – this?* written heavily across them. 'Old Mother Wellington's at it again,' the postman used to announce when he delivered her holiday greeting; and when we did try to get Annabel a foal – a fine old caper that turned out to be, too, what with her measuring fifty-four inches round the waist (Annabel, that is); collapsing in the lane telling us she could Go No Further, it was her Condition, when we tried to get her to exercise; and keeping us on the hop for three months waiting for a late delivery when in fact she wasn't having a foal at all – a good few people thought we'd been brainwashed into it by Miss Wellington, when what we'd hoped for was a small companion for Annabel.

Now, Mrs Binney being otherwise occupied in lurking behind her curtains watching for Mr Tooting, it was Miss Wellington who popped up at the front gate just about every time I put my nose outside to tell me what a beautiful little cat dear Shantung was, what a lovely mother she was sure she'd make, and what wonderful companions the kittens would be for me.

I recalled the one and only litter we'd ever bred: Sugieh's, consisting of Solomon, Sheba and the two Blue Boys who, with Solomon as their self-appointed leader, had terrorised the valley so many years before. Playing ring-a-roses round the chimneys high up on the cottage roof because in those days, before we'd had an extension built on at the back, it had been possible to jump from the hillside across to the sloping roof of the single-storey kitchen and thunder in a miniature posse up to the ridge.

I remembered Solomon, who couldn't climb for toffee though he considered he was best at everything, going up the damson tree at the front gate by sheer force of impetus and falling on the head of the Rector, who never came to visit us after that without pausing at a distance to stoop and peer up into the tree to be sure that Beelzebub, as he called him, wasn't up there. Solomon going up a pine tree on the hillside by the same sheer force of impetus when chased by a dog. Right to the Top, Sugieh had always told them, and right to top he went, and had to be rescued by the fire brigade, clinging to the topmost branch like the Christmas star and bawling the valley for help. The lot of them, chewing holes in socks and blankets, fighting, falling in the water-butt and in their food, constantly demanding More like a detachment of Oliver Twists.

I couldn't stand that again, I told myself. Not my own. Nor could I stand having eventually to part with the kittens, which was the main reason we'd decided against breeding any more in the early days. It had been too much of a heartbreak parting with the Blue Boys, and hearing later that one of them had been run over made us feel like murderers for not having kept them all. Tani wouldn't have a keepable number, that I could bet. With my luck she'd have eight or more, they'd all chitter in chorus when I used the typewriter and I'd go round the bend.

So at six months she was spayed, and apart from Miss Wellington not speaking to me for several weeks and Saska spitting at Tani when she came back from the vet's, saying that she Smelled (next day, as she was full of beans, I put them out in their garden run to enjoy the sunshine, but we had a sudden summer storm and as I passed their run en route from the garage there was no sign of Tani, obviously comfortably ensconced inside the cat-house, which she loved, only of Saska sitting in the open run in the pouring rain announcing that he Wasn't Going In, she Smelled and he wouldn't ever sleep with her again)... apart from one or two vicissitudes like that, all was peaceful at the cottage.

FOUR

It didn't last long. Miss Wellington took on a family of doves somebody over in the next village didn't want and chaos broke out once more at the top of the hill.

Given a picture of a pink-washed cottage with lichened roof and lozenge-paned windows, a garden full of lavender, hollyhock and roses, and an elderly lady in a straw hat standing in the middle with a white dove perched on her hand, most people would have said that, for them, was the epitome of rural England. Alas, while that was exactly how Miss Wellington's garden did look, with her raffia-flowered hat adding just the touch needed for the right old-world atmosphere, the snag was that her cottage overlooked the lane, and she'd had the dovecote fixed between her two front bedroom windows. The birds took to their new home at once, but instead of fluttering lovingly down to sit on her hand among the hollyhocks they spent most of their time stumping about in the road, picking up grit and holding up people wanting to drive past.

Wherever they'd come from they'd obviously never experienced a road before, and had no idea of the danger. They just pottered about playing Who's Afraid when vehicles came along. Practically every time I drove up I had to get out of the car, shoo them away and then rush to nip past before they settled again, and one day I saw the coalman standing in front of his lorry furiously waving a sack at them while Miss W. screeched up and down the scale about his having No Soul, absolutely No Soul, and in future she'd get her coal elsewhere, and he said she was ruddy well welcome, and the pigeons just went on walking about.

The climax came when Mrs Binney happened past one morning and stopped to ask Miss Wellington 'What be goin' to with they, then?' which was one of her stock remarks and actually related to nothing except her desire to start a conversation. Fred Ferry, who lived opposite Miss Wellington and happened to be leaning on his gate, promptly bawled 'Turn 'em into pigeon pie,' and guffawed so loudly at his own joke that he really did scare the doves, who rose into the air in a panic-stricken flurry and made for the dovecote, and in the rush one of them had an accident on Mrs Binney's violet hairdo.

Fred Ferry slapped his knee and nearly fell down laughing, Mrs Binney bellowed something she'd certainly never learned at the Mothers' Union, Miss Wellington said that anybody who used language like that was no lady, and Mrs B. departed in high dudgeon.

Later that day, with the cottages at the top of the hill glowing golden in the evening sunshine and the doves once more pottering about in the road, a car turned the corner by the Rose and Crown and drove slowly along the road past the farm – so slowly it was hardly moving. As it approached Miss Wellington's cottage a hand came out of the window and quietly lobbed something on ahead.

There was an almighty bang, the doves erupted in all directions, and the car came down the hill, turned at the bottom where I was peering out of the window wondering what on earth had happened, and proceeded unhurriedly back up again. There were no doves on the road when it passed Miss Wellington's. Fred Ferry said they were still going round up in the air. Not a bird was hurt. Apparently it had been nothing but a noisy firework. All the cottagers had rushed out, though, and recognised the car and its occupant as it went by, and I heard that Bert Binney came in for a good few free pints at the Rose and Crown that night. And on subsequent nights, because the doves never ignored a car again. Miss Wellington was livid, but she couldn't do anything about it – except pass Mrs Binney with her head in the air when she met her in the village, and as Mrs Binney was doing the same when she saw Miss W. that, as Father Adams said, made two of 'em.

It had been Fred Ferry's fault in the first place, of course, for laughing that outrageous laugh. Like a ruddy hyena, as Father Adams so often remarked. It was, rather. I'd often heard it myself and longed to dot him one, following some ridiculous remark he'd made about the cats. I felt like that when I was taking them for a walk up the Forestry path one night. I'd chosen my time carefully – immediately after supper, when there weren't likely to be many people about with dogs. Saska was on his lead, to which he was quite accustomed. Tani was on one too, for her first expedition outside the cottage boundaries: a light elastic collar with a cord attached, which I'd made by way of training her and also so that I could pick her up immediately if we met a dog, rather than have her bolt in some irretrievable direction.

She wasn't too bad on it. She squirmed a bit and tried to wriggle out of it backwards, but we'd got almost as far as the Forestry gate and she was just beginning to walk properly on it when we happened upon the Smell.

It *was* a smell, too. About half an hour earlier a rider had come down the hill on a strange horse, tried to get it across the stream to go up into the forest, and it had started playing up. Some horses are like that about water crossings they don't know. It had backed, reared on its hind legs and frothed at the mouth. One must never let a horse get the upper hand, of course. Give in to it, turn away, and it will never cross that stream again. So the rider dug her heels in, I went out and made a noise walking behind it, and the horse capitulated and went across... where, to relieve the tension, it did a pool the size of our garden pond in front of the Forestry gate, shook itself, snorted, and went on.

Only in extremity will a horse relieve itself in the roadway. It prefers the straw in its stable, or will move off the bridleway on to a grass verge rather than get splashed. Tani had never met such a spectacle before, but she obviously realised what it was. Anybody would, by the overpowering pong. Her only previous experience of such matters was when Saska performed, and presumably she thought this was one of his efforts – which, being a boy and careless, he hadn't been too careful about positioning. So there we were. Me standing by an enormous wet and pungent patch in the dust, Saska obliviously ahead on his lead tugging to get through the gate, and Tani like small mouse on a string behind me, scratching furiously to try to cover it up.

I tugged the cord, but she wouldn't come. I couldn't go back to her, with Saska pulling hard in the other direction. At that moment Fred Ferry swung briskly down the hill behind me and rounded the corner (Fred was always appearing like that, knapsack on his shoulder and heading for the hills, which was why he had the reputation of being our local poacher) and said, his eyes like saucers, 'Cor did *she* do that?' He knew very well she couldn't have done, but it didn't stop him reporting it as a fact up at the pub, so that people kept coming past for days asking was it true that I had a cat that widdled like a water-cart?

They used to stop and watch to see if she'd perform, and she didn't like it. She would run indoors and hide behind the sofa, protesting that the White Slavers she was always expecting had caught up with her at last.

Life had its complications where my Aunt Louisa was concerned, too. Now nearly eighty, in her young days she'd helped my grandmother bring me up, and I looked on her as my responsibility. She still lived in the old family house in Bristol and, with a strong strain of independence, kindly neighbours and myself keeping an eye on her, she managed very well indeed.

'Managed' was the operative word. She was lively as a cricket, looked about sixty, and ran local affairs, as my grandmother had done before her, as if she were the Queen Mother. Her particular friend was a much younger woman who lived a few doors away and whose name was pronounced like mine but spelt Dorine.

Every day, while Dorine was at work, Louisa would go down to let her two cats, Norton and Petal, into the garden for exercise, get them in again in due course, and generally see that all was well. Dorine, in turn, came up for a chat with Louisa every evening and acquainted her with what was going on in the rest of the road and her own activities, which were not inconsiderable. To help cover the expenses of her big old house, in addition to her full-time job she regularly took, as boarders, two or three students who were on special courses at the nearby polytechnic. They had their lunch at the college and went home at weekends, and thus fitted in well with Dorine's own schedule. She gave them comfortable accommodation, had only to provide them with breakfast and an evening meal five days a week and she and Louisa monitored their welfare between them. Louisa, for instance coped on the odd occasion when she went down and found one of the students still in bed, suffering from a cold or a stomach ache and needing cosseting. Dorine dealt with the reprobate who said he didn't like cats and was caught one day aiming a kick at Norton. He was reported to the college and transferred forthwith to other accommodation. Even so, when I found one of Louisa's pantry shelves loaded one day with bottles of tomato ketchup and Louisa said she was hiding them from Dorine's students, my mind did boggle slightly. Dorine had, it seemed, come up the previous evening breathing fire and slaughter, clutching a bagful of bottles and declaring that this lot (her current quota of students) were really the end. They wanted tomato sauce on everything – even the gourmet meal with wine which she gave them once a week when her boyfriend came to supper – and she wasn't going to have it, so would Louisa keep them for her so she could say with truth that she didn't have any in the house?

She added vengefully that she'd put an air-freshener in their bedroom and they'd been searching for that, but they hadn't found it and never would. She'd put it there because one of them smoked heavily and the bedroom smelled ghastly. Why had they wanted to find it? Louisa asked. Because they didn't like the smell of it, said Dorine. Where had she hidden it? In the smoker's mattress – there was a little tear in the cover and she'd put it inside. Louisa telling me all this, was practically crying with laughter, never realising how peculiar, at times, her own actions were.

Another of her neighbours, Edward, was a bachelor of about my own age. I had known him since we were children, and after his mother died he had turned part of his house into a very comfortable flat and let the rest. He had a daily woman to clean for him; Louisa kept a motherly eye on him and made him cakes; and Dorine, as another remunerative sideline, did odd bits of washing and mending for him. So I was considerably taken aback one day when Louisa said that Edward had asked her to ask me to dye his bathroom curtains for him. Pale blue towelling they were, but they'd got rather washed out. He fancied them a dark brown and he'd be very grateful if I'd do them.

Why hadn't he asked Dorine? I wondered. Was it...? We were about the same age and now both alone in the world... But no it couldn't be, I told myself. He was a confirmed bachelor; I certainly wasn't interested and Louisa knew it. So, out of friendship, I did them. Actually I was quite good at dyeing things: Louisa had probably mentioned it to him, I decided. And the curtains turned out beautifully.

I took them back, Louisa and I went across to the flat and hung them while Edward was out, and I drove beatifically home with the thought of a good deed well done – only to have Edward ring me as soon as I got in, apologising so profusely I could practically see him sweating on the other end of the line. He couldn't understand why Louisa had asked *me* to dye his curtains. 'Never would I have dreamt of it,' he kept protesting. 'Never would I have dreamt of it.' He had meant her to ask Dorine down the road, he explained, and why on earth she'd thought he meant *me*...

I could understand it. Our names sounded the same, and if anyone was going to misconstrue a thing it would be Louisa, who spent her life confusing words and pronunciations. It was around that time that England played the Cameroons in a World Cup football match and Louisa kept enthusiastically telling me, and everybody else she encountered, that she'd been watching the match against the Macaroons on television. She also persisted in calling rudbeckias rudybeckias, referred to her newly acquired microwave, in which she constantly produced her most ghastly failures, as her microphone and generally pulverised the English language in a manner that reminded me of my grandmother – her mother – who, when I was young, used to speak of Hitler as Herring Hitler and Stalin as Old Stallion. Funnily enough, Louisa had never done it when she was younger. Was it a family trait that developed with age? I speculated apprehensively...

I sorted out the confusion of the towel-dyeing, anyway – to my satisfaction if not entirely to Edward's, who went on apologising every time we met for weeks – and returned to my chief preoccupation at the time, which was to see whether I could get the two cats used to the caravan with a view to one day taking them with me on holiday.

When Charles was alive we had planned to do it with Saska and Shebalu. We never got as far as actually taking them. We did try a few days' practice camping in our own caravan field, but that proved so disastrous, and confirmed our neighbours' impression that we were odd even for this village to such a degree, that we eventually abandoned the idea. But Saska was older now, and Tani was such a timid little thing, and I, on my own, would find them such good company on short holidays (I imagined, seeing in my mind's eye the three of us strolling along the sands of my favourite Cornish cove and curled up reading cosily by lamplight in the caravan at night)... and so I started taking them up to the caravan with me

when I went up to air it. They would sit side by side in
the doorway, gazing out at passing riders like a couple
of gypsy cats – they only needed spotted handkerchiefs
and dangling earings – or Tani would investigate the
ground-level cupboards while Saska, as he'd done in the
old days, would climb up to see whether there was a
way out through the skylight (why, since the door was
open, it was difficult to imagine, but Saska never lost
his penchant for imitating Houdini)... and one summer
morning, when the swathes of grass I kept cut, like an
L-shaped lane, to facilitate towing the caravan in and
out were backed shoulder-high with masses of rose-
bay willow-herb, moon-daisies and golden rod that had
wandered over the wall from the cottage garden, they
disappeared. The cats, I mean. Completely.

I couldn't believe it. One minute I had my head in the
cupboard under the sink checking the emergency candles.
The next, withdrawing it as I did every few seconds
to assure myself that they were still in the doorway, I
realised that they were gone.

I dashed out and gazed wildly round the field. Nothing
but that solid backcloth of vegetation, like an enormous
herbaceous border gone wild, into which they must have
disappeared. Unless they'd gone out to the lane... I rushed
to look along that. There was no sign of them. Back to
push like a frantic swimmer through the rose-bay willow-
herb and golden rod towards the line of trees and rising
hillside at the back, wildly calling their names, but there
was no sign of them. They could have been a matter of
feet away but in that tangle I wouldn't have seen them.
On as far as the trees themselves, up and running along

the barer hillside, where there were still tracks trodden flat by Annabel. Nothing. But I knew, there would be adders about in the sunshine. Seeley had, as a kitten, been bitten by one up there. I stamped heavily as I ran, to scare them away, and tried not to think of it. On, everywhere I could think of, but there was no sign of them.

In the end I had to give up searching and wait in the cottage with all the doors open, hoping that they'd come home by themselves. They always did, Father Adams had said when I met him down in his part of the lane while I was hunting. They don't always, of course. Seeley had gone out that morning all those years before and never been seen again. So when blaming myself for taking my eyes off them for even for a second, wondering where they were and what had befallen them, I turned away from the kitchen counter where I was half-heartedly making a cup of coffee an hour later and saw them marching one behind the other towards the sitting-room door without so much as a glance at me, I couldn't believe it. Where had they been? I demanded, falling on knees to scoop them up and hug them. Just looking around, according to Saska, who was the lead as usual, trying to give the impression of having hardly been away five minutes. Keeping an eye on *him*, according to Tani, who was marching hard on his heels. Gosh, I wouldn't *believe* where he'd taken her.

I jolly well would. I decided that taking them away in the caravan was out, and made up my mind to watch them even more closely from then on. And what with doing that, and answering letters, and observing events in the valley, the summer passed.

I was getting more letters than usual. *Waiting in the Wings* had recently been published, and so many people were writing to tell me that it mirrored the way they had felt after losing someone dear to them, or a beloved animal. The book had helped them, they said, and many of them went on to recount their own stories of strange occurrences that had led them to believe that the people or animals they had lost had survived physical death and were waiting for them somewhere on the sidelines.

The incident that impressed me most happened when I was talking to a woman at a meeting in London – a down-to-earth no-nonsense type who was in the legal profession and bred Siamese cats as a hobby. She, too, told me how much she'd liked *Wings* and I told her I'd thought that she, of all people, would think I was batty. 'But it did all happen,' I assured her. 'And my husband really did see Solomon's ghost.'

She believed it, she assured me, looking straight at me. She was certain that people, and animals, went on. She was sure that when any of her cats died, or had to be put down their spirits stayed with her for several days before they left her. She could sense them. There was only one who hadn't, she said, a Siamese male whose original owner had died. When, many years later, the cat had to be put down because of an incurable complaint, he'd only stayed with her for about an hour.

'But why?' I asked. 'Where do you think he went?'

'After all I'd done for him,' she said mock-indignantly. 'Off to find his original owner, of course.'

It wasn't like that when, a year after I lost Shebalu, Saska died too. I had no sense of his staying near me afterwards. All I knew was one of the greatest friends I'd ever had, the last of the animals I'd shared with Charles, had gone, and Tani and I were alone.

FIVE

Saska was only eight when he died of an obscure stomach tumour. My then vet, unable to track down what was wrong with him, had referred him to the Bristol University School of Veterinary Science at Langford, not far from home. They have a special feline research station there which diagnosed a bacterial infection of the colon, but that turned out to be a red herring. By the time the real cause of his illness revealed itself nothing could be done, and he had to be put down.

It hit me as I had thought nothing ever could again after Charles's death. In the end, feeling absolutely flattened, I went to my doctor and she, knowing me, slapped shut her prescription pad and said 'What you need is another Siamese kitten. As soon as possible.' So I came straight home and rang Pauline Furber.

Once again Pauline had no kittens available herself, but there was a breeder at Yeovil whose queen had been mated to Pauline's Bardy, Saska's half-brother. The kittens were ready for sale and Pauline and I went down to see them.

When we were ushered into the sitting-room in Yeovil, there, as one comes to expect in the homes of Siamese breeders, were kittens hurtling in all directions. Up curtains, over chairs, falling like plopping plums through the tops of table lampshades and charging in a yelling, furry posse around the floor. An elegant blue-point queen was strolling about in the midst of the mêlée, ostensibly bawling for order but if I knew anything about it probably egging them on. There was also a large child's playpen lined with chicken wire against one wall with a chicken wire lid and, in a cage on a board across one end of the lid, an African Grey parrot which was sitting against the bars with its head cocked sideways down at the kittens saying 'Go on, then! Go on! Go on!'

He'd helped bring up the kittens, said the breeder, and seeing my glazed expression – I'd heard a lot of odd Siamese stories in my time and met a lot of odd Siamese owners, but this, I thought, took the biscuit – she explained. She had a part-time job and, when she was away from home, she put the kittens and their mother in the playpen so they couldn't get into trouble. It was never for very long and the parrot was good company for them. He talked to them and they nattered back. 'Especially that one,' she said, pointing at a solid-looking young seal-point who was zooming round the room at a rate of knots, batting the rear end of one of his blue-point sisters as if she were a hoop. He, she said, spent a lot of time, even when he wasn't in the playpen, sitting on top of it, close to the cage, conferring with Sinbad.

'Sinbad?' I queried.

'The parrot,' she said. I nodded as if that explained everything.

It possibly did. There was one brief interlude when the kitten stopped batting his sister, belted across to me, and sat studying me with eyes of the most vivid blue I have ever seen, even in a Siamese. Then, loudly encouraged by Sinbad to 'Go on, then! Go on!' (it was his favourite remark, the breeder told me), the kitten climbed my leg, sat on my lap and peered into my face, and I knew that he was mine.

I brought him home with me and introduced him to Tani who spat at him as a matter of principle, walked past as if he was of no consequence at all and completely ignored him after that. He ignored her, too. He didn't hide from her, as she had done with Saska. Kittens brought up by a parrot called Sinbad obviously knew no fear, and he strutted round the cottage as if he were a pirate kitten wearing an invisible bandana and cutlass. He sealed the resemblance a morning or two later when he met up with one of the village postmen.

He was a hefty young man with a big black beard, a gold hoop in one ear and riotous black curls on which he never wore his postman's hat. Altogether his appearance was quite intimidating and he didn't have much to say to people – just handed them their letters or put them through the box. On this particular morning his red van arrived while I was in the top garden with the kitten,

and, as I ran down the path past the cottage to collect
the mail, the kitten – I'd decided to call him Saphra as
he was the son of Sapphire, but he'd already acquired
the much more fitting name of the Menace – dashed
ahead of me and round the corner into the yard with a
swoosh. My first thought was to hope that the postman
wouldn't frighten him. My second was that meeting up
with Blackbeard might teach him not to rush to greet
people he didn't know. I rounded the corner at a gallop
myself to a sight I could hardly credit, the postman was
on his knees, my letters dumped anyhow on the paving
stones, and the Menace was standing on his hind legs
with his front paws on the postman's chest. The two
of them looked at each other admiringly. 'Like to come
home with me? asked the postman. He wouldn't mind.
Could he ride in the Van? enquired Saph.

It certainly didn't make him more careful about meeting
people. The following Sunday Louisa came to see him.
Dee, my cousin who usually brings her out, was away on
holiday, so I drove into Bristol to fetch her. When we got
to the cottage we came in by the back , so that we could
use the kitchen as a Davy escape hatch, closing each door
behind us in as we went through to the sitting-room.

By this time the kitten and Tani were the greatest of
friends. She'd missed Saska; Saphra, by his very nature,
was completely bomb-proof; and they'd accepted each
other more quickly than I'd ever known cats do before.
So I'd left them together in the room, with the stairs and
hall to play in and the hall door shut to safeguard the
sitting-room ornaments – and when I opened it wide,
said 'Here he is – the Menace', he entered, not as a kitten

darting through with fun in mind, but as the Head of the Household, advancing, small spike tail raised like a personal standard, with complete insousiance to meet his guest.

Tani was nowhere in sight, but I knew where she was. Upstairs, on the far side of the bed, sitting on her usual act of hiding under the valance in case the kidnappers had come to carry her off. He, however, marched down the middle of the room like royalty progressing along a red carpet, straight up to Louisa who, tearful with delight, fell on her knees to hug him. 'Oh, the little darling!' she said.

A good many people fell on their knees and called him darling when they met him for the first time. They didn't know what he was like behind the scenes. On his first day at the cottage he'd climbed the bureau by hauling himself up its carved front by his claws, knocked a wooden statue of a prancing stallion off the top so that one of its legs came off, and knocked over a china model of a Breton spinning woman so that her head came off as well (though admittedly that had been stuck on, years before, after a charge by Sugieh's kittens. One gets used to these things with Siamese). On his second day he'd climbed the back of a tall carved chair reputed to be genuine Stuart and rather valuable, stood on the top of it to reach a picture which he also tried to climb, and fallen down in a heap with the picture. And on his third day he fell in the fishpond, which was a sign that he now Belonged. Ever since the time of Solomon, who'd chased a hare through it almost as soon as it was built, all our Siamese boys had fallen into the pond in their early days.

Charles had constructed it in the middle of the yard, between the back door and the side gate, and while I'd prophesied that it would regularly catch the postman or the milkman, all it had caught so far was Siamese cats. Usually when they were chasing something, and they only did it once. After that they avoided it.

But Saphra did it twice. The first time by accident, while out with Tani. I say by accident. Surely she couldn't have egged him on to do it deliberately? The fact remained that they'd come down the garden path together under my supervision after their morning outing and had gone across the yard and round behind the toolshed, where there was a stone outhouse for storing logs, which required regular examination to see who'd been visiting it during the night. Badgers did, I knew. I'd often found badger pawprints, like baby handprints, on the log-house floor.

Anyway, knowing where they were I'd nipped into the kitchen to lower the heat under their rabbit saucepan and had gone straight out again to find Saphra in the yard looking like a drowned rat. I guessed where he'd been. I went across to check – and there, sure enough, was a large splash-mark by the side of the pool and the water still moving where he'd clambered out of it. I looked for Tani and found her sitting in the log-house, busy thinking. Nothing was Anything to do with her, said her expression.

'Well, you won't do that again, will you?' I said, carrying him in the kitchen and wiping him down. But next day he did do it again, and this time I saw him – heading for log-house corner and taking a diagonal short-cut through the pool to reach it. He quite possibly went in initially by accident, but he paddled the strokes necessary to get to the other side like a water-spaniel. And while Tani may have encouraged him to do it, when I looked for her she was once more sitting innocently in the log-house thinking. Where on earth had he Been? she enquired when she saw him. Couldn't leave him for a Second, could she? So in case he had done it deliberately, on the premise that all pirate kittens swam, I hunted out the netting we used to put over the pool to keep passing herons from taking the fish and reinstated it. The Menace, finding that outlet closed to him, turned his mind to higher things.

He started to climb everything out of doors that he could find. Up trees, up gateposts and on one occasion up Mrs Binney. She still came down occasionally to keep an eye on things, but not nearly as often as before the providential advent of Mr Tooting, and this was the first time she'd seen him. I took him to the gate and lifted him up to meet her and in an instant, his gaze fixed on her eye-catching hairdo, he had scrambled on to her shoulder and up over her head, and was sitting on top poking his paw down the violet curls. 'Forward little beggar, in't he?' said Mrs Binney, which was really quite amiable coming from her, and when I'd untangled him from her hair she patted him.

He started to climb the wire netting run of the cats' garden house from the outside too – it was a good six feet high, on a bank on a raised base, and he'd shin up and dash about on the wire top like a mad thing. Which was all very well – I was always on hand to lift him down from the slope of the cat-house roof when he'd had enough – until the day he and Tani were watching a mousehole in the stone at the top of the lawn. I'd slipped in to take something out of the oven (I had to do things like that when I thought they were safely based a moment) and when I scurried out again they were missing.

I called them. No response. I blew Charles's scout whistle which I kept in my pocket for such emergencies – I'd long ago discovered that when I blew it Tani, always expecting the kidnappers, would emerge full pelt from wherever she was and bolt for the cottage. But, this time she didn't. The lawn – and it was almost dusk – was bare and silent. So I dashed inside for the only thing I could think of – the tin of cat biscuits that to both of them was a summons to heaven – and ran up the garden path rattling it. As if by magic Tani appeared from somewhere at the back of the cottage and rushed indoors and Saphra, too, shot across my vision. Not at ground level but darting across the top of the cat-run and, in order to get to the cat biscuits before Tani, launching himself from above my head out across the path and plonk down on the lawn on the other side.

It was a good eight-foot drop and I started to run again, sure he must have hurt himself, but he bounced up fresh as a daisy and came tearing towards me. Pirate kittens did things like that, he informed me in a Siamese bawl. That was his Boarding Jump. Sinbad had taught him about it. Now what about those biscuits?

A few days later he did far worse than that. It was a Sunday evening, and as usual I'd been out on the lawn with them. I'd picked up Tani and carried her in because it was supper time and gone back to fetch the Menace, whom I'd left studying a beetle in the border. Always ready for a game, he put his ears back, raced across the lawn and shinned up the tall plum tree against the garage wall. Right to the top from which he stepped off on to the wide, gloss-painted strip that edged the sloping garage roof, and immediately lost his footing on it.

The garage is a conversion of a 250-year-old barn, the same age as the cottage. It is some twenty feet high at the apex and the roof-slope is steep. He couldn't get a grip on the painted wood, it didn't occur to him to jump beyond it on to the rougher tiles, and he started to slither down towards the bottom.

'No... please!' I breathed, unable to do a thing to help except hope I might be able to catch him when he fell off. Then one of his claws caught in a splintered bit, he held on there for dear life anchored by one paw and yelling at him not to move, I rushed down to the woodshed for a ladder. He couldn't have known what I was saying – he hung there because he wasn't able to move – but the result was the same. I belted back with the ladder – fortunately of light aluminium, and I managed to extend it easily – slapped it against the roof and scuttled up it. He wouldn't let me unhook him with my hands, but clung to the wood strip for all he was worth. Only when I lay flat against the ladder and put my shoulder under his back feet, so that he could get a grip with them, did he turn and clamber cautiously down my body, sinking his claws into me like climbing pitons every inch of the way. How he would manage when he got to the end of me I dared not think. At that point, however, he was a good way down from his original mind-boggling height and was level with the top of the Bramley apple tree on the other side of the path. One leap and he was across the gap and sprawled flat as a starfish across a branch of his haven.

Hurriedly I scrambled down the ladder and grabbed him before he could find anything else to climb. I'd thought I was alone while all this was happening. I should have known better, of course. No sooner did I start down the path, one hand firmly clutching Saph's scruff, the other under his feet, holding him against my cheek because, despite the fact that he put years on me with every day that passed, he was Saska all over again and I loved him dearly, than 'You shouldn't let him do things like that – he might hurt himself' came a voice from the now darkening shadows of the lane.

I recognised it at once. Miss Wellington. If it had been Mrs Binney, after all the tales I'd been hearing – mostly from Fred Ferry – about her being seen around the country lanes at twilight with a companion in a pork-pie hat, I wouldn't have been so surprised. But Miss Wellington? What on earth was she doing out and about almost in darkness?

SIX

I soon found out. Miss Wellington, having revealed her presence in the lane, obviously thought she'd better explain why she was there before the rumour went round that she, too, was having secret assignations in the gloaming.

It seemed that her sister, widow of a headmaster and herself recently retired as headmistress of an infants' school in Wiltshire, had bought a cottage which was for sale further up the lane from me and was shortly moving into it. I'd mentioned the cottage to Mrs Binney as a possibility for Bert, but she said Shirl was a town girl and din't fancy living up among all them trees, whereas mine was in a spot where there were more people about and had a proper road running down to it. Shirl wanted her own car when they got settled, she said importantly.

Which took care of Shirl, and why Miss Wellington's sister wanted to live in such a remote spot, up a side lane off the main one, with a very rough stretch of bridle path to drive over before she got to it and, if it came to that, close to Miss Wellington, was anybody's guess. But she did want it, and had bought it, and Miss Wellington was keeping a self-appointed eye on it. To see that vandals didn't damage it before Poppy moved in, and dusk was the time when they were most often about, she told me, which left me with two thoughts uppermost in my mind: first that from now on I could expect Miss Wellington to be hovering in the lane any time I was in the garden at twilight; and second that if her sister's name was Poppy what on earth could Miss Wellington's own Christian name be? I'd never heard her referred to as anything but Miss Wellington. If I'd been asked to hazard a guess I'd have said something like Augusta or Victoria with that surname. In fact in the fullness of time, when Poppy Richards had moved in and started to refer to her sister in conversation around the village, we discovered at Miss Wellington's name was Pansy. Before long the two sisters' cottages – one at the top of the hill and the other up the valley in the other direction – were known as Pansy's and Poppy's, and Miss Wellington had become Old Pans when spoken of by the more disrespectful locals such as Fred Ferry, while her sister needless to say became Old Pop.

This is jumping ahead of events, however. For weeks before Mrs Richards moved in Miss Wellington was as consistent a visitor to the valley as Mrs Binney had been, lurking around like MI5 at dusk, marching through proprietorially during the day, picking up loose stones from the bridlepath on her way up to the cottage in case, she explained, she turned her ankles on them; and snapping off odd sticks and branches in the hedge on her way back in case, she said, they scratched her sister's car when she moved in. The stones she dumped on the grass verges of the lane which, as I owned the land on both sides of it, were mine, and I kept the grass on them cut down with the hover-mower and from then on was forever catching the blade on the stones with a horrible scraping noise and using language about Miss Wellington that would have shocked the Rector. The branches she tossed into the wood on her way back up the hill – always at the same spot. The wood, too, was mine and the collection was starting to look like the beginnings of a Guy Fawkes bonfire. I didn't like to say anything to her, but the air was rapidly becoming electric.

There was also the question of the lawn at Poppy's cottage. It was June, and the grass was growing fast. Miss Wellington mowed her own small patch with a hand-mower but she couldn't possibly cut her sister's much larger lawn that way, so she engaged Ern Biggs to do it, thereby putting another foot firmly through the sacrosanct crust of village etiquette.

Once upon a time Father Adams had been the village odd-jobber, but he was now too old and rheumaticky to do more than potter round his own garden. Fred Ferry regarded himself as the old boy's natural successor, but Fred, never seen without the mysterious knapsack over his shoulder, reputed to be given to overcharging mightily for any job he did, wasn't everybody's choice, and when

Ern Biggs, who lived in the next village, was invited to do some gardening by a newcomer who'd met him in the Rose and Crown one day, and his reputation for doing a fair job at a passable rate got round, quite a few people – newcomers themselves, who didn t know about village etiquette – switched to him. Now he had become as familiar a sight around our village as if he belonged to it.

Miss Wellington had always coped with her own small garden and its population of concrete gnomes and toadstools herself, and when it came to Poppy's property, if there was anybody she wasn't going to employ it was Fred Ferry. Not only did she disapprove of the implications of the knapsack and of his rolling home singing from the pub at night to his cottage practically opposite hers, but once, when there'd been a spate of break-ins in the village and Miss Wellington, scared of being burgled herself, had been seen bobbing about behind her hedge with a trilby hat on a stick – presumably to give would-be intruders the impression that there was a man about the place – Fred had seized the opportunity to start the story that she had a fancy man, and he knew who it was, and Miss Wellington had never forgiven him.

To Fred it was all a joke. Starting rumours is a traditional country pastime and nobody took much notice of his fabrications. But when Miss Wellington, who'd lived in the village as long as anybody could remember (though she hadn't been born here: her family had been a county one, with a big house some miles away, but she and her mother had moved here when she was a young girl, after her father died) when *she* so far forgot village propriety as to employ Ern Biggs to do her sister's garden, things, in Fred Ferry's eyes, had gone beyond the pale.

He went round looking daggers every time he saw her and gazing pointedly in the opposite direction when he passed Poppy's cottage. Ern hadn't helped matters by copying an idea he'd picked up at one of the big houses, where a contractor had put a board outside reading ALTERATIONS BY W. BROWN. Ern now carried a board which he put outside places where he was working which read GARDEN BY E. BIGGS and seeing it outside Poppy's place was like a red rag to a bull to Fred.

Fate having its own idea of fun and games, the next thing was that Ern slipped one day while mowing the steep hillside lawn at Poppy's cottage, broke his ankle and was off work for several weeks. At that point Miss Wellington had no option but to humbly beg Ferry to take on the garden as there was no-one else and Fred accepted. The first thing he did on taking over was alter the wording on Ern's board so that it read GARDEN BY E. BIGGS PUT RIGHT BY F. FERRY. And Miss Wellington, unable to find anyone else to do the work had to put up with it. Father Adams likewise went on record as telling a visitor who looked over his wall, saw his rampant row of raspberries and asked whether he took orders, that he was British and didn't take orders from nobody, and so the summer moved on.

With it progressed the catastrophe-filled kittenhood of Saphra, abetted by Tani. One of his earliest accomplishments was to break an old oil lamp with a blue glass bowl and engraved shade which I'd treasured for years. It was set, deliberately out of reach of the cats, high in an alcove at the back of the sitting-room. Saph was hiding in a newspaper tunnel on the carpet while I dangled a piece of string enticingly at the opening when Tani, to show she knew he was in there, jumped on the tunnel from behind with all her might. He exploded out of it like a snooker shot, straight across the room, up the wall and into the alcove. He stayed there with his fur on end, the lamp fell out and smashed, and all I got in reply to my anguished wail asking why he had to do that was an answering wail to the effect that he was more important than an Old Lamp, wasn't he, and Somebody had tried to Get Him. Tani had meanwhile vanished discreetly under the sofa.

In the same week he got into the glass cupboard in the kitchen while my back was turned and broke two sherry glasses (I saw them sail horizontally out of the cupboard as if by magic) and the very next day, tore ahead of me down from the cat-house when I was bringing them in at feeding time, and round the corner into the kitchen, whence came the immediate sound of smashing china. When I panted through the door he was eating his chicken off the floor out of the remains of the broken dish.

Next, having once more unthinkingly left their dishes on the cooker top while I fetched them in (it had never been necessary to take precautions before), I followed behind to find him standing up there bolting food out of one dish with his feet in the other while Tani bawled from below that she'd Smack Him if she was me: he didn't have any Idea of Manners.

Then he rediscovered the fascination of water. I found this out one day when I wondered where he'd gone and did my usual panic patrol round the cottage, opening doors and looking in cupboards. Rushing through the kitchen for the umpteenth time I happened to glance at the sink and there he was, a small seal-masked figure like a furry highwayman, sitting in it absolutely entranced, watching the drips, completely oblivious of the fact that as they fell they bounced off his outsize ears. After that, when I followed Charles's practice of watering special plants in the garden with rainwater from one of the butts, he would rush after me when he saw me with the watering can and follow me round assiduously. Straight from the spout or falling gently through the rose, it was all the same to him so long as it was water and he was watching it.

Out of doors, when he wasn't following the watering can he was usually on the heels of Tani, whose turn it now was to look fed up when he jumped over her, or pounced on her tail, or spoilt everything by poking an excited paw into a hole in the wall that she'd been sitting patiently in front of for ages. At least I knew where he was, though, when I saw the snake.

Leaving them together in the long grass at the edge of the lawn one morning, I'd gone up to the area beyond the garage where Charles had been in the process of building another conservatory. It was roofed with perspex sheeting, and the stones he'd been using for building the walls were still heaped underneath; until I could get round to clearing it out I used it for dumping things under shelter and I'd gone up to fetch the hoe I'd left there the previous day. As I went in, wearing sandals on bare feet, avoiding the nettles that had grown up between the stones, I felt a sudden warmth against one ankle. Saphra rubbing against me, I thought. But no, I remembered. He was on the lawn. It was my imagination. I went on without looking down, picked up the hoe, turned to come out – and saw, where I must have brushed against it going in, a large coiled snake lying sunning itself on the ground. It wasn't an adder. It was too big and it hadn't the diamond markings – but if there is one thing I don't like it is snakes.

Saphra! I thought in alarm. Any moment he might come whizzing round the corner and pounce on it, scenting a plaything. And supposing it *was* an adder. Their markings and colourings do vary. There are black adders up on the higher hills.

I leapt high over the snake, still curled, apparently asleep, and ran down the path. All was well. Saph was still on the lawn with Tani, his small cream and brown figure sitting importantly upright alongside her elegant, slender ice-white one. I grabbed him, hurried him to their run, rushed back for Tani, thrust her in with him and fastened the door. I went back to check on the snake's markings, but it had disappeared. It hadn't been asleep. It had seized its opportunity to slip away into the stone-pile. It couldn't have been an adder, I told myself. But I'd keep a weather eye open all the same.

It was July before I saw the next one, and despite my watchfulness it turned up in the cat-run itself. Jeanine McMullen, author of *A Small Country Living* and presenter of a country programme of the same name on the radio, had come to do an interview with me and we got on like a house on fire. Jeanine herself runs a small farm on the side of a remote Welsh mountain and is fond of cats, and we had much in common. We exchanged hints on looking after cottages, and Jeanine recorded stories about the animals Charles and I had had, and our life in the valley. We were standing in the garden at the end of the interview when, microphone in hand, she looked across at the cat-run and said, 'Do you think the cats would talk so I can record their voices?'

Sure, I said. A reader from South Africa and her husband had brought some biltong as a present for them the previous week. Biltong, which is sun-dried deer meat, once formed the travelling rations of the South African pioneers; today it is sold there in small bags, like potato crisps, and eaten as a snack. The cats were mad about it. I'd only have to wave the bag in front of their run, I assured her and they'd be yelling their heads off.

So I fetched it and crackled the bag at them, but they took no notice: simply sat there some way back from the wire netting front of the run, facing each other and concentrating on the ground between them. 'They've got something live in there,' I said. 'Probably a slow-worm. I'll go in and rescue it.'

So, I unlatched the door and went in, but it wasn't the grey, metal-smooth skin of a sloworm that met my eyes. It was a brownish back with diamond markings, lying in a crack between the paving stones.

'An adder!' I yelled, leaping into action. Tani was sitting back from it, keeping a wary distance, but Saphra was crouched within inches, one paw raised to hit it if it moved. I grabbed him, rushed to the cat-house at the other end of the run, threw him through the door and latched it. I ran back and grabbed Tani, intending to do the same with her. Jeanine was in the run herself by this time, intent on helping me. She'd field Saphra, make sure he didn't rush out when I put Tani in, she said. Only it didn't work like that. As I put Tani through the door, Saphra erupted through the cat-flap at the bottom of it like a circus rider coming through a hoop. Back to watch the adder he streaked, and I streaked after him, leaving Jeanine to stop Tani from getting out. I ran down to the cottage with him, put him in the kitchen and dashed back with a box which I up-ended over the adder, still down in the crack between the stones, while we got Tani down to the safety of the cottage too. It took some time because Tani, hiding behind one of the deck-chairs stacked in the cat-house, had to be hauled out, screeching up and down the scale like a banshee.

Frightened by the adder? That was what I imagined, grabbing her by the scruff and rushing her down the path still wailing like a set of demented bagpipes. Jeanine and I then went back to deal with the adder, but when we picked up the box it had gone. Out through the wire netting into the long grass behind the run, we decided, and it wasn't likely to come back. Tani's howling had been enough to frighten off an elephant. When we went back to the cottage, however, to make some coffee to restore our nerves, and Tani started up again, we realised it wasn't the adder she was protesting about. It was Jeanine. A stranger who'd had the temerity to intrude into Tani's Very Own Cat-house: her Refuge when Danger Threatened. And had it threatened! Tani bawled balefully from under the sofa. If she hadn't done her Defensive Call the kidnappers would have Got Her.

It was at that point that Jeanine realised that her microphone, attached to her belt, was still switched on. The entire incident had been recorded. Tani's screaming opened and closed one episode of 'A Small Country Living', while the recording of our rescuing the cats formed part of it. People listening to it probably thought she was warning off the adder. What she was really doing was warning off Jeanine.

That wasn't the end of it, either. After Jeanine had gone I cut down the long grass behind the cat-run and laced a foot-deep length of heavy polythene right round the wire netting to stop the adder coming back again, though after Tani's performance it was probably in a hole somewhere having a nervous breakdown. Later events were to show how wrong I was.

For days I kept constant watch over the cats, going up regularly to check that they were all right in their run and listening, when I wasn't near them, to be sure nobody was screeching a warning. Thus, a week or so later, I came to be on the other side of the cottage from the cat-run, chopping down brambles in the lilac hedge that bordered the lane and stopping every now and then, as I couldn't see the run from that point, to listen to make sure all was well.

Suddenly I heard the sound of hooves approaching and a voice I recognised booming out her latest achievements in horse-breeding. Not wishing to be caught – it was, I knew, a local female, accompanied by her much-henpecked husband, who would keep me talking for ages about her latest foal if she saw me – I got down on my hands and knees and took refuge under the hedge, only to hear the woman bawl, as she neared the gate, 'What on earth's that noise?'

'Don't know,' replied her weary spouse.

'Somebody's calling,' persisted the woman. Then, answering her own question, she announced, 'It's one of the Siamese on heat.'

'Thank goodness horses don't make that noise when they're on heat,' said her husband with feeling.

I couldn't hear any howling with the cottage between myself and the cat-run, but Tani had been spayed... it must be another adder. I erupted from under the hedge, much to the couple's astonishment, and tore up the path – to find the two cats side by side, tails bushed like flue brushes, swearing horrible oaths at the ginger cat from up the lane, who'd come down to sit outside their run and tantalise them about being Shut In like Cissies.

SEVEN

That story soon went the rounds as further evidence of my eccentricity. 'Mrs Haskins be tellin' people thee'st come up out of thic lilac like a Jack-in-the-box and frightened her hoss near out of his wits,' Fred Ferry informed me happily later. 'What wust thee doin' on thee hands and knees anyway?' he enquired hopefully.

I wasn't telling him, but neither was I surprised to learn that I was being talked about. I always had been, ever since I'd been seen in the garden shortly after we moved to the cottage with our tame squirrel sitting on my head to get a better view of his surroundings, and Father Adams assured me that he'd told the person who'd seen me that I wasn't as daft as I looked.

From then on there'd been a succession of incidents for people to mull over. When *Cats in May* was published, for instance, a television crew had come out to the cottage with the idea that Solomon and Sheba were going to climb out of transom windows, carry things round in their mouths and walk welcomingly out of the front door, on either side of me, as I'd described in the book. What actually happened when they had an audience, as any Siamese owner could have forecast, was that Sheba disappeared completely for the duration of the visit and Solomon, after one look at the camera, dived into a clump of delphiniums in the flower border and refused to come out. In the hope of encouraging some action I tied a kipper to a piece of string and, long after Charles and the camera crew had given up and retired to the cottage for refreshment, there I was, jogging round the lawn trailing it behind me, with no sign of a Siamese cat anywhere – just me, an empty lawn, a kipper on a string and, as I suddenly realised, the local riding-school teacher and her retinue of pint-sized riders watching me open-mouthed over the wall. Once I'd given up, of course, and retired indoors covered in embarrasment, Solomon emerged from the delphiniums and started prancing about with the kipper like Nureyev – but the riding party had long gone by that time, the camera crew packed up, and all that remained of that episode was the legend, oft recounted in the Rose and Crown, of me and the kipper on a string.

It was the same when we acquired Annabel, our donkey. Me being towed down the lane on my bottom when Annabel was supposed to be hauling wood. Me trying to give rides with her at the village fete, and Annabel going determinedly in the wrong direction. And, remembered in the village to this day, the time Charles and I were going to a music recital and Annabel went missing.

We didn't dress up very often. Neither our lifestyle nor our inclination subscribed to it. But the recital, a charity affair, was being given in a stately home, and proper gear was de rigueur. So the cats were indoors, the car was waiting in the drive and Charles and I were dressed. All that was necessary was to put Annabel in her stable for the night with her bowl of apples, carrots and bread – a task made easy by the fact that she normally followed Charles, who always gave her her supper, at the trot, with her head in the air like the Bisto Kid. We'd left her up on the hillside till the last moment because it was a summer's evening, the sun was still shining, and it seemed a shame to put her in before we had to. Then out went Charles, shaking the bowl to attract her attention and keeping a weather eye open to make sure nobody saw him in a dinner jacket – only to discover that the gate to Annabel's hillside grazing ground behind the cottage was open and she was nowhere to be seen.

Goodness knew who'd opened it but we couldn't go off and leave her roaming at large. It would be after midnight before we got back and Annabel, not in her stable after what she considered to be her bedtime, was apt to bawl the valley down telling the neighbours about it. Equally certain was the fact that Charles wasn't going to be seen hunting the highways and byways for her in his get-up. So who charged up the hill in gumboots and floating chiffon skirt hauled up to the knees, a bridle in one hand, Annabel's supper bowl balanced precariously in the hand holding up the skirt, enquiring of every passer-by whether they had seen her?

I did, of course, and nobody had. She wasn't at the local farm, where she stayed when we went on holiday, or up in the pub yard where she could be sure of plenty of attention any time she played truant. I got the attention instead.

I trundled back down to the cottage, where Charles was reversing the car into the lane so we could search for her further afield, and suddenly spotted her up on the hillside, coming through a gap in a thicket in the far top corner, where there was a path that ran behind two cottages further up the lane. She hadn't run away. She'd been along there all the time, spying on the neighbours which was another of her favourite occupations; hadn't deigned to come back because she was Busy, and now was ambling back for supper in her own sweet time, supremely indifferent to the fact that we were going to have to drive hell for leather to get to the recital and that I, chasing around in wellies and evening dress clutching a bowl of bread and carrots, was going to be the object of head-tapping in the village for weeks.

If I had thought, however, that things had changed – that with just me and the two cats at the cottage my image was going to subside into one of quiet, cat-companied sobriety – I soon discovered my mistake. I had far more to do now that I was on my own – weeding the borders, weeding the paths, pruning the fruit trees, cutting the lawn-edges – and, to make the best of my time, I hit on the idea of doing such jobs while I was out with the cats. It worked. It is amazing how many weeds one can pull out of a section of path, or leaders one can cut off an apple tree with long-handled pruners, in five minutes while keeping an eye on a kitten. The snag was, it usually was only five minutes. Tani

I had no need to worry about. She never went outside the garden, and if ever I lost sight of her I only had to blow Charles's scout whistle and she would reappear, streaking at the speed of light for the cat-run and into the cat-house where she considered that Nobody, not even Kidnappers, could get her.

Saphra, growing up now and not so inclined to tag at her heels, was a different proposition. One minute he'd be on the front path with her, peering down a mousehole while I pulled out some weeds. Next moment he'd have upped and offed to the top border to dig a hole and I'd be up there with him, discreetly cutting a piece of lawn-edge. As soon as he'd finished that (and hole-digging was an art in itself as far as Saphra was concerned: he'd excavate down to his elbows before the hole was deep enough, sit on it, flood it to overflowing and turn round to examine it, his very own contribution of that most interesting substance, water, in wondering detail before covering it over with a long-distance paw as if such things were nothing to do with him)... as soon as he'd finished that, tail up, feeling a New Man, he'd belt up the steps by the garage, round the corner and along the drive, and I'd be after him, cat-crook in hand, to stop him going out under the gate.

The cat-crook was home-produced. Years before, cutting down undergrowth in the wood opposite the cottage, I'd bent down a tall hazel rod that was too thick to cut with shears and was impeding my way. Some two years later I came across it one day when I was again clearing the ground up there. The rod was now about an inch and a half thick and some six feet long, with a hook where I'd bent it over at the top. A natural shepherd's crook, I decided, and sawed it off at the base, brought it back to the cottage, trimmed it, dried it out and varnished it. A fine support stick it make for rambling over the hills, and useful protection for a woman on her own, or in the garden for seeing off dogs that threatened the cats through the gate, or for fielding one fast-growing young boy cat with ambitions to be an explorer. It fitted exactly round his neck and, extended from behind, reached him across distances which I, with just my hands, couldn't have spanned.

He knew when he'd been foiled. He'd reverse out of the crook and come back to sit watching for anything that might move in the row of raspberry canes – where I, dropping the crook and picking up the three-pronged fork I kept at the side of the garage, would weed at top speed for a moment or two until he moved on again.

Logical when one knew the reason for it, and I got through a lot of weeding that way, but it was a source of considerable speculation to casual passers-by. Not so casual eventually. I began to recognise the same faces, gathered two or three together or in Fred Ferry's case on his secretive own with the mysterious knapsack on his shoulder, gazing over the wall in wonder as I darted hither and thither, picking up a tool, scratching the ground with it, then throwing it down and sprinting like mad to some place else, always clutching my shepherd's crook.

'Never keeps at any thin' for long. She's always on the run like that,' was one comment I heard.

'Sad how gets 'em, innit?' was the reply. 'But she always was a bit queer, wun't she?'

'Whass she got thic crook for? Reckon she's goin' in for sheep?' reached my ears on another occasion.

Well, I wasn't. And I hadn't replaced Annabel, either. I'd thought of it, but Louisa reminded me of the winter nights when Annabel had colic and Charles and I had to hold her up between us and lead her up and down the lane by torchlight till she recovered, with her sagging dramatically to the ground at every opportunity.

'You could never do that on your own,' said Louisa, and she was right. Neither could I be sure of getting a donkey that was colic resistant. So I gave up the idea, and the grass in the field beyond the cottage, where I kept the caravan, grew long with nobody to eat it, and I had to keep it cut down with the hover-mower so that I could drive the car in to hitch up when required, and when I found that riders were getting into the field through the gap at the far end, cantering down the mowed section and jumping the pole across the entrance into the lane, I got annoyed. The horses' hooves made deep indentations in the surface that became a quagmire when it rained and, in dry weather, a rocky, pot-holed area that was hard on the car's suspension. When I found the pole broken one day I'd had enough. I put up a notice saying that the land was private property and that riders jumping horses or ponies in it were trespassing and would in future be prosecuted without further notice.

The result was amazing. This was years after the incident of Solomon and the kipper. By this time there were two riding schools in the village and several more, from neighbouring villages, who came over to trek in the forest, and the day after I put up the notice the girl in charge of one party appeared at the cottage door to apologise for the fact that two boys who rode with her had been going regularly into the field and jumping the pole. They'd ignored her instructions not to do it, she said, but now they'd seen the notice they were scared of being prosecuted and she'd come to plead on their behalf.

I wasn't going to prosecute anybody, I told her. The notice was just to keep people off, and I didn't suppose those two were the only ones who'd been doing it. Well, she'd told their mother about it, she said, and she thought I'd be hearing from her. With which, vastly relieved to hear that her riding school wasn't about to appear en masse in a magistrate's court, she departed and the next thing was a call from the boys' mother apologising for their behaviour, saying that she'd stopped their riding for a week, had told them she'd sell their ponies if they did it again, and felt terribly embarrassed about what they'd called me.

'Called me?' I echoed. 'But I've never spoken to them. I don't know your boys – and I'm sure they aren't the only ones who've been jumping in there.'

Their riding teacher had told her that they'd sworn at me, she insisted. Had actually repeated what they'd said, and she wasn't having them use that sort of language to anybody. She was sending them to apologise in person, and would I please tick them off thoroughly when they came.

That evening two small boys appeared, each clutching a shop-wrapped sheaf of flowers which I guessed had come out of their pocket money. Eyes down, avoiding looking directly at me or they'd have realised I wasn't the person they'd sworn at, they apologised, said they'd never do it again, and shot off up the hill, obviously glad to get away without being clapped in jail.

I never did find out who it was they'd sworn at. Probably Miss Wellington, I decided. I could imagine her remonstrating, in her role of protector of the valley, with anybody riding rough-shod over my field. What I couldn't understand was her not telling me about it. Always ready with what she'd said to people and what they'd said to her was Miss W. Always keen to be seen upholding the right. I can only imagine the language they used was such that, being a lady, she couldn't repeat it. I've always longed to know what it was.

Summer also brought the visitors – readers who, passing through Somerset en route to Devon or Cornwall, wrote to ask if they could come to see the cottage and the cats. Most of them hadn't seen Tani before, and were upset to hear that Saska had died. But all of them were entranced by Saphra – the way he welcomed everybody as his friends – and all of them were intrigued by Tani, who would hide for ages on a chair tucked under the big oak table, come out eventually, when she saw Saphra getting all the attention, to rub against a hand or two herself, and then, in the middle of being made much of, would creep across the carpet, flat on her stomach, and take refuge on her sanctuary chair again.

'Why on earth does she do that?' people would ask.

'She thinks you're white slavers,' I would explain solemnly – much, I feel sure, to Tani's satisfaction. 'She's always expecting somebody to kidnap her.'

She was, too, and one day the pair of them gave a memorable performance. I'd made tea for the visitors – a couple and their two young daughters – and brought in a plate of biscuits to accompany it. Saphra adored biscuits and the girls gave him one on the carpet straight away. One bite, of course, and there were better things to do to attract attention – like racing round the room, hurtling along the back of the sofa on which the visitors were sitting, diving to the floor with a mighty plop, then doing it all over again. Everybody was laughing, everybody was watching him. Saphra got quite carried away, and when, on one of his wall-of-death circuits, in diving off the sofa he landed on his abandoned biscuit and it scattered in smithereens, he was overcome by the merriment he caused. They put down another biscuit and round he raced again, leaping off the settee to land on it deliberately, the fragments flying, and the light of supreme achievement beaming from his small black face. Tani meanwhile, unable to bear his hogging the limelight, kept venturing out from under the table to watch and then, having successfully drawn all eyes to *her*, putting on an act of Realising the Danger she was In, dropping flat and crawling stealthily back to her chair.

'Like to be the centre of attention, don't they?' said the husband, nearly dropping his teacup as Saphra, zooming along the sofa-back behind him, hurled himself off on to yet another biscuit.

They certainly did. That, I remember, was a Monday. By Wednesday, with me in panic-stricken attendance, Saphra was the centre of attention at Langford, under suspicion of having eaten a purple towel.

EIGHT

When Saska was at Langford under observation I had asked the vet who was treating him whether there was a nearby practice that specialised in small animals. The local vets I knew of dealt chiefly with horses and farm animals. For years I'd been driving my cats on a round trip of fifty miles when they needed attention, and it was a long journey: I'd done it on occasion in snow, ice and fog, and a cat expert nearer home would be a blessing.

To my surprise the vet told me that Langford had just opened its own Small Animal Practice. Hitherto they had only accepted animals referred to them, as Saska had been, by a vet baffled as to diagnosis. But they had recently taken over the practice of a local vet who had retired, and so long as the animal needing treatment wasn't on the books of another vet in the district it could now be taken direct to Langford.

My previous vet being such a long way away, my cats qualified at once. Tani went there when her loose stomach recurred. She was prescribed special bran to be mixed with her food and never suffered from nervous diarrhoea again. (Nowadays they recommend cooked rice mixed with the food, and that achieves the same result.) Saphra had been neutered there... made much of by the staff, but I did wonder why the senior professor, who also presided over the evening surgery, carried him out to the car when I fetched him that night. Was he glad to see the back of him, and if so why? I wondered. And now there was the episode of the purple towel...

Siamese cats are given to chewing things, and Saphra was no exception. First it was tea-towels, red and white checked ones. He chewed the corners off them any time he could contrive to be on his own in the kitchen, and I used to turn cold at times when I looked at his litter tray and wondered what dreadful malady he'd developed, until I realised it was only the tea-towels taking their normal course and gave fervent thanks that they had. Then he discovered the purple hand-towels, also belonging to the kitchen, that hung from a rack over the washing machine.

Sitting on the latter he could reach them comfortably, and apparently they were just the job for filling hungry corners. Before long every purple towel I owned had a pair of parallel holes halfway up it, to the limit of kitten-sitting level, and when I hung them on the line after washing people had even more cause to stare when they went by. They looked for all the world like a row of Ku Klux Klan masks.

Then, the Wednesday after his exhibition of jumping on the biscuits, Saphra went off his food. He sat about looking worried, didn't want to go out and eventually disappeared. I searched everywhere I could think of, including the space between the side of the freezer and the wall in the kitchen extension which Saphra, odd-minded cat that he was, had adopted as his private lair. Situated where it was, near the back door, I think his main idea was that if I didn't know he was there I might leave the back door open and he could get out. But he would sit there for long periods meditating, as well. So I looked, and he wasn't there either, but something was. A long, mysterious something which, when I hauled it out, turned out to be a purple towel, half of it eaten away.

Whether he'd had it there for some time as reserve rations or had eaten it at one sitting I didn't know – he could have taken one out of the kitchen cupboard at any time – but the moment I did find him, sitting behind the bedroom curtains and looking wanly out of the window, which was quite out of character for him, I rang Langford, told them what had happened and they told me to bring him over straight away.

Getting the car out, putting a cat in the carrying basket, tearing up the hill at panic stations – I'd done it so many times before. But this time it wasn't a matter of twenty-five miles to go. Ten minutes and Saph was on the surgery table. The teaching professor sounded his heart, felt him all over, took his temperature. That was up a bit, he said, but there didn't appear to be much wrong. He'd give him an antibiotic injection. Would I bring him back next morning and, if his temperature as still up then, they'd do an X-ray. He paused, looked at Saph, who was looking back at him with the most penetrating of sapphire stares, and seemed to remember something. On second thoughts, he said... seeing it was him... they'd do an X-ray anyway.

What did he mean? I wondered. Was he remembering Saska? Or had Saphra blotted his copybook when he was neutered there?

I took him home again. Back to the cottage. He didn't want any supper. But later, in the garden with Tani, with me standing by, worrying myself sick about what the next day might reveal, he stage-managed something that was absolutely typical of him. Suddenly darting across to a clump of ferns he caught, with one swift pounce, a mouse. A baby mouse which he brought across, dumped on the grass in front of me and then, as I bent to retrieve it, grabbed and tossed tantalisingly in the air. It flew sideways and through the mesh of the wire netting round the cat-run. Hoping it was still alive I dashed into the run after it – only to see him, on the path outside, toss his head again, and another mouse flew through the mesh and landed at my feet. He must have caught two at once. True, they were only babies – he must have found a nest – but only he could have picked up two at once. 'Waaah' wailed Tani disgustedly when I asked her what she thought of it, which I took to mean that he wasn't half a show-off and we shouldn't encourage him. He certainly was, I agreed, and told myself there couldn't be much wrong with him, prancing about like that – but he still didn't want any food.

So there we were next morning in the X-ray room at Langford, the veterinary nurse and I in lead-lined aprons and Saphra stretched out on the table between us. I imagine I'd been asked to assist on the premise that my presence might stop him from being scared, but there was no fear of that. 'Now we're going to see whether your sins have caught up with you, young man,' the nurse said with mock severity. Lying on his side, confident that everybody was his friend, he regarded her with wide-eyed equanimity.

The X-rays taken, he was put back in his basket and I was asked to sit in the waiting room while they were developed. It was just my luck – I had been full of equanimity myself until then – that while I was sitting there someone came out of an adjoining room, left the door open, and through it I was suddenly aware of two white-coated figures examining an X-ray plate. They were holding it against a light. It *couldn't* be Saphra's, I told myself, though I knew it most probably was. 'I wouldn't *think* that was a growth,' I heard one of the viewers say. I would, at that moment. I'd heard the uncertainty in her voice. I was going to lose my boy the same way I'd lost Saska, I thought, my heart sinking like a stone. Realising that the door was open, somebody closed it. I heard nothing more. A little later, someone came out and said the X-rays had been inconclusive. They were going to keep him in, give him a barium meal and watch its progress. Would I like to go home and ring around mid-day?

I did. Nothing had happened, I was told when I rang. There was something there – at junction of the colon and the rectum. But it wasn't moving. Could I ring again in two hours' time? I did. Still no news. Could I ring in at five o'clock?

At five o'clock they said they wanted to keep him overnight and I rang off sick at heart, convinced I was going to lose him. Tani, talking her head off, was busy shadowing me everywhere, being my Faithful Companion. I have noticed that she does this when she is the only one around. Whether she was missing Saph, or taking advantage of his absence to bring herself to the forefront whereas normally she took second place and occupied herself with her fantasy of kidnappers I don't know, but she went with me to the kitchen, to the bathroom, jumped on the freezer and lectured me while I bolted the back door for the night, stood on the bed and talked to me, tail in air, while I undressed, and curled in my arms and purred like a bumble bee when I lay down, though normally she slept downstairs with Saphra. She was sitting by me on the hall chest, still talking away, when I rang Langford next morning. Whatever it was appeared to have moved slightly, they said. Could I ring again at mid-day? The bulletins being issued about Saphra, as if he were royalty, would have pleased him had he known, I thought. Possibly, being Saphra, he did.

It was a Friday, when I always went to Bristol to see Louisa and help her with any jobs she wanted done. I would ring from there, I told them. At mid-day they said could I ring at three and ask for the professor, who would like to speak to me himself. Sure, once more, that I was going to hear bad news, I had to sit down to make the call at three o'clock, knees knocking together, while Louisa stood by with a glass of brandy. Whatever it was was on its way, reported the professor to my relief, but it was taking a long time. Would I mind having him home for the weekend and watching progress? He didn't seem to like their arrangements, he added in what I thought sounded a hesitant voice. Oh, Lord, what had that cat done *now*? I wondered. But at least he was coming home. Louisa drank the brandy herself when I told her.

The professor asked me to collect Saph before the five o'clock surgery. He would explain matters when I saw him, he said. It was just after four when I left Bristol, and as I drove out of the city I noticed groups of people congregated along the roadside. At first I wondered what they were waiting for, but then the penny dropped. The Queen had been in Bristol that day, opening a hospital extension. She was due to leave the airport just before five. This was the route to the airport and people were gathering to see her. Schoolchildren. Guides. Scouts. They stood there ready with their flags. A Guide grinned and waved her flag at me. The girl next to her waved and cheered as well. In a flash the whole line was cheering. Goodness knew who they thought I was but I entered into the fun of it, waving back with one hand and bowing graciously as I drove. The cheering and waving spread. I wondered what the royal party must be thinking if they were at all close behind me. For me, though, it was an occasion for celebration. I was going to collect Saphra who, diabolical though he was, had installed himself so dearly in my heart. I waved and bowed all the harder.

When I got to Langford, I found that the reason the Menace was being sent home – expelled, if one looked at it squarely – was, the professor explained, that he wasn't co-operating. Wouldn't use his litter tray. Had only used it once since he'd been there, so how *could* anything come out? And his bladder was fit to burst he said, feeling Menace's stomach gingerly with his eyes raised to the heavens. I knew at once why it was, but I thought I'd look silly if I explained. I used pine-needles from the forest in Saphra's litter and he wouldn't have anything else. And it had to be changed after every sitting – he wouldn't use a litter tray twice, however large it was. I didn't suppose they had time for that at Langford.

So I brought him home, and Tani was pleased to see him, and he headed for his litter tray and performed at once, a relieved expression on his face. It took until Sunday for anything of note to appear, however. Something that looked like a miniature Catherine wheel, about the size of a 1p piece, and I recognised it straight away. A piece of the fringe off the rug in the hall, coiled tightly round and round.

The professor had asked to see anything that transpired, however, so I put it in a box addressed to him personally, added 'from Saphra' by way of identification and took it over to Langford on Monday morning. Only afterwards did I wonder what his staff had thought, opening what must have appeared to be a present from a grateful cat. Probably by that time both Saphra and I had been written off as odd, I decided. Certainly there wasn't a modicum of surprise in the professor's voice when he spoke to me later on the phone, to tell me he didn't think that could have caused the trouble. They didn't know what had, but he was sure there was nothing wrong with him now. I needn't bring him back again, but would I contact them immediately if I was worried.

I watched like a hawk, but all was well. The only thing I learned from my observation was that Saphra had invented something. Was it, I wondered, the result of having been, if only for a short while, at such an august seat of learning?

It was the following day and it was raining. The cats were in their garden house with their infra-red heater on while I got on with some work. I went up to the garage to get some papers from the car and as I passed their run the flap in the cat-house door lifted smartly and Saphra's face appeared out of the opening. He didn't come out. Just watched me go past with the flap resting flat on his head, keeping off the rain. It wasn't an accident. He did it again when I came back from the garage, peering out with the complacent expression of being perfectly protected from the elements. Saphra had invented a cat umbrella.

I was astounded by his cleverness, and equally bemused by something else that had happened around then. Readers of *Waiting in the Wings* may have remembered that after Charles's death I'd gone into the legend, told me years before by my father-in-law, that his family was descended from Tovi Pruda, standard-bearer to Canute. I'd found out a great deal about Tovi, including the fact that Waltham Abbey, in Essex, is on the site of a church originally built by him alongside one of his hunting lodges.

I also learned that in 1042 he'd married Githa, daughter of another Danish nobleman called Osgod Clapa, at Lambeth – and that Canute's successor, Harthacanute, had died suddenly while drinking a toast to the bride at the wedding feast. Harthacanute was only twenty-three years old, wasn't very popular, and one wonders what dark deed lay behind the happening. Tovi doesn't seem to have been implicated, however. He and his descendants continued as standard-bearers to the kings of England down to the time of the Norman Conquest, when Tovi's grandson Esegar was Marshal and Staller (the equivalent of High Constable of England) to Harold, fought with him at the Battle of Hastings, and was the only one of the king's retinue to survive it, dying in London three months later.

After the Conquest all the Tovi lands were given to William's henchman, Geoffrey de Mandeville, and the family faded into obscurity, but it was a story that completely fascinated me. My own family goes back a long way, but we have nothing on Charles's history, and when Gemma, one of my cousins-twice-removed, came, with her husband, to stay with my cousin Dee that summer, and Louisa and I went to supper with them and the talk turned to family history, I couldn't resist telling them about Tovi.

I hadn't met Gemma before. It was Dee's side of the family that had kept in touch with hers, and Dee had told me that Gemma wasn't terribly bright. Apparently it was taken for granted in Gemma's own highly intelligent family. Once, Dee told me, when she was staying with Gemma as a child, Gemma had rushed to her mother complaining that Dee had called her a fool, and her mother had replied tartly 'If Dee says you're a fool then you must be.' Even I, though, was at a loss for words when, after I'd conjured up for them a picture of the wedding at Lambeth – Tovi looking, I imagined, rather like Charles: tall, nordic-featured, green-eyed; Githa blonde and slender as a lily in girdled, sweeping white silk; Harthacanute and his nobles carousing lustily (No doubt wearing, in Gemma's imagination, helmets with whacking great horns on them, though actually Viking helmets didn't have horns at all) – Gemma leaned towards me and asked eagerly 'Have you got any photographs?' I was completely stunned. It was quite some while before I could close my mouth and point out faintly that photography had not been invented then. 'Ask a silly question and you get a silly answer,' said Gemma, serenely. I still haven't worked out that one.

NINE

That was the summer I decided to sell our sailing canoe and started another local rumour. The canoe had hung, unused, from its pulleys in the garage roof ever since Charles's death, and though I hated the thought of parting with it I was also afraid that one day the ropes would give way and it would fall down and damage the car.

So I got one of my neighbours to help me lower it, and we carried it down to the lawn so that I could clean it, and unwittingly put it just where it caught the eye of everybody coming down the hill. A graceful sixteen-foot two-seater, sails, mast and paddles on the grass at its side: half the village appeared at one time or another to speculate as to why it was there.

Mrs Binney was the first to actually ask me. She hadn't been down for quite a while, but the news had obviously reached her by local grapevine and she must have decided it meant I was moving at last.

'What be goin' to do with that boat, then?' she began, leaning on the gate to watch me varnishing the decking.

'Sell it,' I replied.

'Gettin' ready to move? she queried hopefully.

'No,' I said. 'It's just a pity to leave it in the garage unused.'

'Don't forget my Bert'd like to know when you *are* goin',' she continued single-mindedly.

''Tis too big for you.' The cottage she meant. 'You wants one of they little bungalows up Fairview.'

A little bungalow up on Fairview was the last thing I wanted, but Mrs B. obviously thought she was sowing a seed of thought in my mind and, patting her violet curls, she stumped back up the hill, having imparted a piece of information of her own that she was also patently anxious I should know. The Friendly Hands Club was departing on its communal summer holiday at ten o'clock the following Saturday morning, this time to Edinburgh. She was going, she announced. So was Stan she added coyly, peering at me from under her eyelids to see whether I was impressed. I was impressed, all right. Stan, she'd said. Obviously she meant Mr Tooting. In all the years I'd known her she'd never referred to her husband, alive or defunct, other than as Mr Binney. Things certainly did seem to be moving.

This I must see for myself, I thought. So I made sure I was in the post office on Saturday morning when the coach arrived in the square ready to observe how our village siren operated. It was simple really. The coach drew up and the passengers gathered to go aboard, Mrs Binney determinedly at the front of the queue. She climbed the steps, subsided heavily on the seat just inside the door, dumped her holdall next to her and leaned back and closed her eyes – firmly, so that the availability of the vacant space brooked no question from anybody until, when the coach was full, Mr Tooting climbed aboard (he, as secretary, had been checking everybody on from a list on a clipboard) whereupon Mrs Binney opened her eyes and transferred her holdall to her lap. Mr Tooting had no option but to take the seat next to her – the only one left with nobody in it and where, as self-appointed courier, he no doubt thought he should be anyway. In front, right behind the driver.

Father Adams's wife didn't go on the trip. She wouldn't leave the old boy on his own, and wild horses wouldn't have dragged him on it. She was in the post office too, though – wouldn't have missed it for worlds, she said – and together we waved the coach on its way. 'Looks like romance, duunit?' she observed, her eyes glued to Mrs B. and Mr Tooting. I wasn't so sure. To me it seemed more like a female spider weaving a calculated web and Mr Tooting falling inescapably into it.

I walked back to the valley thinking that anyway, I had a week's reprieve. Mrs B. couldn't come pestering me about the cottage. Country life being what it is, Miss Wellington descended upon me instead. She hadn't gone on the communal holiday either. It wasn't Miss W's style. What she had done was notice the canoe on the cottage lawn from the top of the hill, ask Fred Ferry if he knew why it was there – he was still cutting the grass at Poppy's cottage and calling at Miss Wellington's to be paid – and he, never one to miss a chance of leg-pulling, particularly when the leg was Miss W.'s, said hadn't she heard? I was going round the world. Taking the cats as well, he added as a bonus.

He'd obviously got the idea from a report in the papers at the time about a man proposing to cross the Atlantic in a barrel. It didn't come off – the authorities prevented him doing it – but Miss Wellington had no doubt read about it too, and the possibility of my trying something equally stupid must have seemed credible to her.

Down she came, the afternoon of the day the Friendly Hands trip went off, when as luck would have it I was scrubbing the sails, spread out flat on the lawn, while the cats, to be companionable, were sitting one in each cockpit of the canoe, for all the world as if they were ready to take off. Our previous cats had often sat in the canoe like that when it was on the lawn for cleaning. There is nothing Siamese like better than being involved in what is going on. It would have been more unusual if they hadn't been sitting in it.

But Miss Wellington rushed through the gate, threw her arms round my neck and burst into tears, causing Tani to bolt for the cottage. Saph stayed where he was and yelled 'Waaah' at her in greeting, but Miss Wellington had other things on her mind. 'Don't do it,' she sobbed imploringly. 'You mustn't do it. Think of the poor little cats.'

'Do what?' I enquired. 'I'm only scrubbing the sails. That isn't going to hurt them.'

It came out then. What Fred Ferry had said. And Mrs Binney had told her Bert was hoping to get my cottage.

And I always had been adventurous. Look how Charles and I had gone to the Rockies searching for grizzlies. But I mustn't think of doing such things now, without him. He wouldn't like it.

I put her right on all counts. I wasn't going anywhere, I assured her. I noticed, though, that when I'd sold the canoe – I advertised it in the paper that weekend and someone bought it the following Monday (a man wanted it to sail with his young son on the Somerset rhines, as Charles and I had done, and I couldn't think of a better future for it) – I noticed that no sooner had it gone up the hill on top of the purchaser's car, its yellow warning streamer fluttering from its stern, than Miss Wellington came pattering down the hill to look over the gate. To make sure I was still there?

That same week, while I was watching over the cats in the garden one morning, a little man arrived who'd been coming through the valley almost daily for quite a time, on what seemed to be a regular walk around the forest. He always stopped to pass the time of day with me and admire the cats. He liked gardening and he loved cats, he told me regularly, while Tani equally regularly fled indoors growling and Saphra, crouching, fixed him with a suspicious look and said he didn't believe him.

He was short, pompous – another Mr Tooting. I found him boring, but he would stay and talk. He was a comparative newcomer to the village and he lived on the Fairview estate – a widower, he informed me. He watched me for a while that particular morning as I nipped about in the wake of Saph, dead-heading a rose here, pulling a weed out there, crook in my hand ready to field the Menace should he try to take off. 'What you need is a man about the place,' he said suddenly in a sympathetic voice, leaning confidentially over the gate.

I nearly jumped out of my gumboots. Was there no peace anywhere? Mrs Binney. Miss Wellington. Now him. So far as I was concerned there was nobody in my life but my tall, handsome Charles. Never had been. Never would be. I hoped he was, indeed, waiting somewhere for me in the wings. Perhaps I misjudged my visitor's intentions, but I wasn't taking any chances. I had no desire to be thought another Mrs Binney. 'I've just acquired a very good handyman,' I told him icily. He stood for a moment, then walked on up the lane. He never came past again.

I had indeed acquired a handyman. His name was Bill, he was an ambulance man, and he did household repairs in his spare time. He lived ten minutes away by car and had been recommended by friends, who said he was a good, quick worker – not like Mr Panting, the awful old man I'd employed before, who dragged every job out to its limit. He didn't charge fancy prices and genuinely liked helping people. There was only one thing, said my friends. Never let him do any indoor decorating. He went at everything at the speed of sound, and if he was painting a door, for instance, he never put a dust sheet or even newspaper on the floor. Just worked away feverishly, splashing paint in all directions, then trod happily and obliviously through it afterwards.

I remembered that. He did a lot of jobs for me but I never let him work indoors. Even outdoors, however, his speed was apt to run away with him. Whatever he came to do he would belt down the hill as if answering a 999 call, leap out of his car, shoot down the path, rope me in as assistant, and within minutes be deep in the job, usually without giving me a chance to change out of my slippers. The first time he came to my rescue was when a length of rotten facing board fell off the apex of the cottage roof, and I noticed a crack in the wall beneath it.

I had called a builder who shook his head and said that was going to be some job. He'd have to bring along his brother-in-law, a roofing specialist, to do it – but he could tell me himself it would entail taking off the overlapping row of tiles, renewing the wooden tile supports, moving the bathroom downpipe to investigate the depth of the crack, filling it in and re-whitewashing the wall. 'And how much will that cost?' I asked, fearing the worst. He couldn't say exactly, he answered. Five hundred pounds. Maybe more. Scaffolding cost a lot to hire.

'Scaffolding?' I echoed. 'Can't it be done with a ladder?' Not with the conservatory built against the wall, he said. It'd need scaffolding to cover the sloping glass roof underneath. *Nobody'd* go up there otherwise.

That was when I went to my friends, who rang Bill for me on the spot. He'd come over the next evening, he promised. I went home and he turned up within half an hour – found he had time before supper so he'd just popped over, he explained. 'Do it this weekend,' he said, surveying the job. 'Got any planks that'd go over that glass?'

The conservatory had been designed by Charles, with stone-built walls front and back and a glass roof sloping down between them. Across the lane, in Annabel's old stable, were five long, wide, three-inch thick planks. Placed side by side on top of the walls they formed a solid platform over the glass. Charles, a stickler for safety, had stood ladders on the platform with complete equanimity when painting the side of the cottage himself. That was why I'd boggled when the builder mentioned scaffolding.

'Ah,' said Bill when I told him. If I could help him across with a plank he'd take a closer look at what wanted doing. Then he'd tell me how much it would cost.

I helped him across with one plank, we raised it and positioned it, and I asked should we fetch the rest. 'One'll be enough,' said Bill airily. I closed my eyes as he leaned a ladder against the conservatory wall, climbed it and got on to the plank. I watched heart in mouth as, sure-footed as a mountain goat, he hauled the ladder up behind him, leaned it against the upper cottage wall, went up it and examined the roof-edge, the woodwork and the crack. Came down, dusted his hands and said the tile supports were solid. All it needed was a new piece of weather-boarding, cement filling, painting and a coat of whitewash. 'Seventy pounds all right for the lot?' he asked.

Was it! I died a thousand deaths as he did the job, managing with only one plank. I nearly did myself a mischief, too, handing up hammers, nails, buckets of cement and, when that was done and dry, mixing the whitewash. But we did it. This was some time back, of course, when prices weren't as high as they are today. But seventy pounds instead of five hundred... Bill was factotum at the cottage from that time on, even if it did mean making more cups of tea than I'd ever brewed in my life. He drank tea as most people breathe. There was also the business of always turning up like a whirlwind, invariably in advance of when he'd arranged, and consistently incorporating me as handyman's assistant. But one can't have everything.

Thus it was that when the septic tank backfired (the outlet blocked, and I couldn't have a bath, and I phoned Bill one chilly summer's evening, and he said he'd only just come home – hadn't had his supper, but he'd be over the next day definitely)... there I was in sheepskin slippers, relaxed for the evening, a quarter of an hour later when Bill zoomed down the lane, screeched to a stop outside the cottage and rushed in asking 'Where's the end of the run-off, then? And where d'you keep the drain-rods?'

Before I had time to breathe he and I, still in my slippers, were heaving the heavy railway sleepers off the top of the pit that Charles had constructed years before on the far side of the lawn so that the outflow pipe from the septic tank could be rodded. One got down into the stone-walled pit, found the end of the pipe threaded the rods along it, heaved them backwards and forwards till the silt blockage began to give – then leapt for dear life as the pit suddenly flooded. I nearly lost my slippers and it started to rain, but we did it, lifted the sleepers back on, laid the drain-rods in the stream to wash themselves clean, and Bill said he'd best be getting back for his supper. I said he shouldn't have bothered, I could have waited till tomorrow. Well, the meal hadn't been quite ready, he said. And he hadn't liked to think of me being unable to have a bath. Now I could go and have one.

I needed one by that time, after battling with the drain-rods, but I didn't like to say so. How much did I owe him? I enquired instead. 'Would a fiver be all right?' he asked.

It would have taken a long time to make his fortune at the prices he charged, but he insisted that he liked giving people a hand. He gave many a hand to me. As fast as he helped restore my peace of mind, however, Saphra seemed intent on demolishing it. I'd never had a cat like him.

It seemed that heredity had something to do with it. Saska, his predecessor, had been dastardly enough. And Saska had inherited his intelligence and Machiavellian ways from his father Saturn Sentinel, Pauline Furber's stud cat, of Killdown descent, who was known for passing his individualism on to his offspring. Saphra's pedigree had had to be sent on to me by post – his breeder had run out of pedigree forms when I bought him. I knew he was a grandson of Saturn Sentinel, and Saska's nephew on his father's side – but it wasn't until I got his complete pedigree by post a week later that I discovered he was also descended from Saturn Sentinel on his mother's side. What I'd got – I wouldn't have changed him for worlds, but I did blench slightly when I realised it – was a kitten with Saska's lineage on both sides. Was Saphra going to be twice as intelligent as Saska had been – and twice as dastardly?

Twice as dastardly seemed to fit the bill. And being brought up by a parrot hadn't helped. There'd already been the business of Langford and the purple towels. And then he went absent without leave.

I couldn't bring myself to put him on a lead. It would have been like trying to harness a grasshopper. Instead I trailed him like a shadow, which took up a lot of my time, though he didn't seem to appreciate the attention. WAAAH, he would complain when I stopped him going out under the gate. Why didn't I go and follow Tani? Because Tani was sitting contentedly on the lawn, that was why – watching a butterfly on a clover flower, and dreaming. WAAAH, he would protest, when I lifted him off the garden wall. The grass was better out in the lane. Why couldn't he have some of it? WOOOH he would howl when, for the umpteenth time, I hauled him down from the cat-house roof from which he had the obvious intention of jumping off on to the hillside behind the cottage and setting off to explore the forest. Couldn't a cat have any Freedom?

The answer was no, so long as I was around. I remembered the awfulness of losing Seeley. The day came, though, when after sitting for ages in front of the clump of ferns by the front gate in case a shrew came out, he jumped up on to the gatepost and from there out into the lane. He'd done it before and had never run away. Just stayed in the lane looking interestedly around until I picked him up and brought him back into the garden, telling him a quarter of an acre was enough for any cat, to which he usually replied with a thwarted WOW and went off to torment Tani.

This time, however, I was just about to pick him up when he crouched flat, looking further up the lane. I looked, too. There was a black and white cat standing, startled, in front of Annabel's stable. Even as I made a grab for Saphra he slipped through my hands, heading like an arrow for the stranger. There was nothing of the Pleased To Meet You attitude with which he greeted humans. It was more like Here I Come With My Cutlass. In a flash the other cat had gone up the wall of Annabel's stable on to the orchard bank and, with Saphra hot on his heels, tail bushed to its fullest extent, disappeared into a sea of nettles.

I couldn't climb up on to the stable wall. The bank in front of it was too steep for a foothold. I had to run further up the lane to the orchard entrance, up a track between the apple trees, and along the overgrown path behind the table until I reached the nettlebed, which looked even more impenetrable at close quarters.

There was no sign of the two cats. Not a single leaf or weed-stalk moved. There was no sound. Why wasn't Saphra howling? His predecessors at the cottage used to wail like air-raid sirens when they met up with another cat. I could always track them by their voices. When any of them got chased up a tree or cornered somewhere, they always used to howl for me to come and rescue them.

Was Saph facing the intruder inside the nettles, where I couldn't see him, and battle might break out at any moment? Was the other cat, which I didn't recognise, hot-footing it for home – maybe miles away – and Saphra at that very moment following after him? Had he lost sight of the other cat and, his mind wandering as Siamese minds are apt to wander, was he ambling off, under cover of the nettles, on some other project altogether? Up to the farm field at the top, for instance, where I could hear machinery clanking – and Saph was interested in anything that moved. Supposing he got too near it?

My neighbours thought I was potty, I knew, to worry so much. Cats always came back, they said. They knew their way home. But Seeley hadn't come back. And I'd heard of cats being killed by farm machinery. And Saph had never been across in the orchard or up the hill – supposing he didn't have a homing instinct?

I did what I'd done for years, whenever a cat went missing. I couldn't go through the nettles – they were waist-high and covered too great an area. So I came back down to the lane and started my tour. Up the hill to the Rose and Crown, left up another hill to the top lane, back along that, looking down across the farm field to check there was no long-legged truant following the hay-mower, and beyond that, peering into the depths of my own wood. Calling 'Saffle-affle-affle', my diminutive for Saphra, as in years past I'd called 'Solly-wolly-wolly' and, to the cat who'd never come back, 'Seeley-weeley-weeley'.

Saphra didn't answer, but other people heard me calling. Fred Ferry, going along to the Rose and Crown, asked 'Cat gone missin' then?' as I passed him, which was pretty stupid as he obviously was, but it did mean Fred would spread the news along at the pub and somebody might spot him later. Miss Wellington came down the hill prodding the undergrowth with a walking stick, which was also still. Saph wouldn't wait there for her to poke him out, but at least she was trying to be helpful. Janet Reason said she'd take her retriever, Daisy, round the lane in the hope of tracking him down, but I didn't think that was likely. I couldn't see Saph coming unresistingly home in Daisy's mouth like a furry, long-legged pheasant.

For nearly two hours I circled that area of land; calling, looking, worrying. Nobody I asked knew of a black and white cat living anywhere in the neighbourhood. The two of them could by this time be miles away. Then, coming past Annabel's stable for the umpteenth time, looking across at the cottage case he'd returned by himself in the meantime, I suddenly spotted him. Ambling down the hill towards me: unhurried, confident, obviously knowing exactly where he was. He reached the bottom of the hill and looked towards me, but instead of coming along the lane to meet me he turned left and started down the other lane, where he'd have passed the Reasons' cottage. But Janet was out searching for him with Daisy and nobody could have seen him, and he'd have gone on to the remoter part of the valley. Was it coincidence that I'd returned at that very moment... or was it because I'd just been silently asking Charles for help? I hadn't asked at first. I only did it when I reached an impasse... and once again it had worked.

I ran after Saph, picked him up, hugged – never, ever, could I be cross with him – and put him into the cat-run where Tani, the perpetual Good Girl, was sitting surveying the world as though he'd never been missed. He rushed up to her, bit her on the neck and said he betted she didn't know where he'd Been. Didn't Care, Either, said Tani, biffing him with a reproving paw.

TEN

She did care. She loved him in spite of his consistently treating her as if he were Tarzan – when, if I was around, she would scream blue murder for me to come and rescue her. Fond of being the Rescued Heroine, was Tani, although when she thought I wasn't looking she often bit him back to encourage him to do it again. He was over-rough with her at times, though, and a vet I knew who was an expert in cat behaviour suggested I should get a water-pistol. He'd used it to cure one of his own kittens who'd had a habit of biting, he told me. It would dissuade the offender, who would associate it with what he was doing when it was pointed at him and would realise it was better not to do it. The water wouldn't hurt him – it was just that he wouldn't like it.

So it proved. The most embarrassing part of the exercise was buying the water-pistol. I can still see the look on the assistant's face when I went into the toy shop and asked for one. 'For my Siamese cat,' I explained in case she thought I wanted to play with it myself, at which her eyebrows went even higher. She knew Siamese cats were odd, her expression said, but she really didn't believe they used water-pistols.

I explained it was to stop a male Siamese from biting his timid companion. She smiled hesitantly and helped me select one. Blue plastic – with a good long range, she said. But she still eyed me somewhat warily.

It worked, anyway. It got to the stage where I only had to point it in Saph's direction and without waiting for the spray, he would stop whatever he was doing and flee precipitately. Fascinated by water he might be, but not when it came at him with that force. I caught him several times, however, examining the water-pistol when it wasn't in use, lying on the bookshelf near my elbow. Wondering whether he could operate it himself, no doubt, but fortunately that was beyond him.

Really, though, they were very fond of each other. Originally, once they'd become friends, they'd slept together on Tani's blanket in the armchair in the sitting-room, but Saphra, deprived of his purple towels, had started chewing pieces off the blanket during the night, pulling it down on the hearthrug to get a better grip and leaving Tani sitting forlornly on the chair arm, where I'd find her wearing her long-suffering I've-had-no-sleep look in the morning. So I replaced it with the Snoozabed set on the hearthrug – without a blanket on it for obvious reasons – and they slept happily on the fur-fabric cover, or so I thought.

Until one night, roused by blood-curdling screams which I recognised as Tani's and wondering what disaster had struck this time, I rushed down to find the Snoozabed disappearing under another chair, Tani sitting upright in the last visible corner of it like the Lady of Shalott going down to Camelot, and Saph under the chair, tugging the Snoozabed backwards with all his might, his teeth sunk in the opposite corner.

What did he think he was *doing*? I demanded, picking Tani up in my arms. It was obvious when I looked at the Snoozabed. He'd been chewing holes in the fur-fabric in lieu of the blanket, obviously tugging the whole thing away to hide for future consumption, and not caring a bit about how much he was annoying Tani, which was probably part of the fun. I dumped the pair of them in the hall, shut the sitting-room door and took them up to bed with me. Better to have them where I could keep an eye on him, I thought. They curled themselves into a combined ball on top of the eiderdown against my back, and settled down for the night. Why hadn't I thought of this before?

It was comforting to wake in the early hours, aroused by somebody stirring, switch on the bedside lamp, look down the bed and see two innocent pansy faces, heads together, looking sleepily back at me – until the owner of the innocent black pansy face got up saying he was Cold, and came and prodded me with a paw to let him under the eiderdown, and the moment he was settled the owner of the innocent lilac pansy face plodded up and prodded me to let her get under as well, and all would be quiet for a time while they warmed themselves, till Saphra would

115

suddenly erupt from under the bedclothes saying now he was Hot and Couldn't Breathe and struggle frantically out on to my pillow, and Tani, saying she was Hot too and the eiderdown was Squashing Her, would struggle out after him, and they'd sit bolt upright by my head till they'd cooled own sufficiently for the performance to start all over again.

After two nights of this I went out and bought a duvet which would lie more lightly on them, with mental apologies to Charles, who'd always resisted our having one saying didn't I remember how in Switzerland they were a foot thick and always fell off and left us frozen... but Charles had never had to sleep with exploding bedclothes.

The duvet was a great success and Saph soon resumed personal control of it. The duvet cover was sunflower yellow, and I put a bedspread over it to stop it getting dirty when they lay on it. Saphra's system was that when it was warm he and Tani slept on top of the bedspread, as I intended. When it got a little cooler, however, he'd stand on my pillow and lift the bedspread gently, with the slightest touch of his paw, as an indication that he wanted to go under the bedspread but on top of the duvet. Bang went the idea of keeping the duvet clean, but if it kept him quiet it was worth it, I thought. So I would hold up the bedspread and he would go under, and I would drop the bedspread over him. Seconds later Tani, who usually sat in the window alcove while this was going on, would pad across my pillow and lift the edge of the bedspread, too, insisting on being let under to join him.

A still lower temperature – say around 3 a.m. – meant that Saph crawled out from under the bedspread and raised the edge of the duvet itself, to show he now wanted to lie directly against me for warmth... followed by Tani crawling out and putting her head under the duvet, so that I had to hold it up again for her.

Once underneath, it was Saphra's prerogative to have First Place, stretched lengthwise against my side – something he adopted as his right. Tani then took up a subordinate position close against him, keeping him warm on his other side. She was so much the complaisant handmaiden on these occasions that I wondered she didn't wear a yashmak. I'm sure Saph would have approved...

After a few nights they expanded the routine to include going downstairs again on some errand of their own before they came back and really settled... a procedure instituted by Saphra, who, after I'd got into bed myself would claw at the closed bedroom door and yell till I opened it, whereupon, followed by the handmaiden, he would disappear down the stairs. After half and hour or so of silence – no fights, no crashes, no yells for help, though I waited anxiously to hear them – up they would come and get into bed, Saph first, Tani behind him, and all would be peace, give or take a wriggle or two, until the following morning.

Curious as to what they were up to, I crept down one night to check. Saph, sitting in the two-foot-deep embrasure of one of the windows overlooking the lawn, looked suitably sheepish at my appearance. Just checking on things, he said. Tani, perched high in the long horizontal window that looked out on the hillside at the back of the cottage, turned her head towards me when I went in, then switched it back to the window again. There were more interesting things outside, it seemed.

There certainly were. Badgers, foxes; I'd found their tracks in the garden, back in the winter when it snowed. Deer, too. There were roe deer in the forest, which came out on to the hillside to graze. I'd pulled back the bathroom curtains one morning and there was a doe right outside the window. She'd stared at me for a moment, then turned and leapt into the pine trees that rose like a backcloth behind the cottage. It was like a stage setting for Hansel and Gretel.

Satisfied, after I'd checked on them, that they weren't up to mischief – only watching wildlife, as was natural for them – from then on I left the bedroom and sitting-room doors open at night so they could go down at will and the sitting-room curtains pulled back so they could look out without hindrance, and they delighted in their freedom of choice. When they did come back upstairs, instead of jumping on the bed immediately, Tani would sit in the bedroom window for a while, staring out at the valley from there, while Saphra did a tour of the room itself, opening cupboards to see what they contained.

That was when the trouble started. The bedroom is small – too small to take a bedroom suite, which we'd replaced by built-in fitments. A low, built-in cupboard in one of the fireplace alcoves, topped by a triple mirror, took the place of a dressing-table. Another long, low cupboard along the wall at right angles to the built-in wardrobe substituted for a tallboy. The only drawback was that, as the cupboards were shallow, there was no room in them for sliding drawers: they had to have shelves and doors.

Drawers would have been difficult for a cat to manage, but opening doors was kitten's play to Saphra. Like Saska before him, he had paws which worked like jemmies – one claw-hook and a tug and the ball-catch clicked back immediately, exposing the contents of the cupboard for examination.

Oh, what treasure was there for a pirate cat! Woollen sweaters to be taken out and chewed – always round the cuffs and welt, so they looked as if mice had been at them. Eventually, in desperation, I transferred the bulkier sweaters to zipped, heavy plastic storage bags and kept them in a cupboard above the wardrobe. The few thinner sweaters that remained intact I put in the bedside cabinet, which did have small drawers, but alas these particular ones proved to be non-Saphra-proof.

I had a thin purple polo-necked sweater, one of my favourites, that I wore one day to a Siamese Cat Club meeting in London. Sitting at the top table with the chairman, delegated to be the next speaker, I took off my jacket because the room was hot, raised my wrist to look at my watch and nearly dropped when I saw, there before my eyes, a large semicircle missing from my sweater cuff. Too late to put my jacket on again – it was time for me to speak. I raised my arm in the air. 'The Menace has struck again,' I began. It brought the house down. All the members there had Menaces of their own and we had a grand time swapping tales about them.

How Saph had done it I didn't know, unless the cuff had been protruding from the drawer. How he got hold of my jewellery, kept on a shelf in the dressing-table cupboard, was on the contrary patently obvious. I could hear him hooking it out during the night. The items were mostly in individual boxes and he enjoyed opening boxes, raking them out with his paw so that they fell on the floor and the covers came off.

He was attracted by anything that glittered, as our first boy Solomon had been. Solomon had once put a set of keys down the clock-golf hole in the lawn and they hadn't been found for ages. Saphra likewise carried his trophies round in his mouth, his initial favourites being a long gilt chain and a gilt brooch fashioned like a feather. The chain I would find on the stairs in the morning, carelessly dropped like spilt pirate booty. The brooch he would hide under the bureau in the sitting-room, pulling it out to play with when he fancied it, particularly when visitors were there, when he was in the habit of walking round like a miniature pirate chief, with a gilt feather sticking out of his mouth. I didn't mind the chain or brooch. They were only costume jewellery. It was when he turned his attention to my earrings that I rebelled. Oval jade earrings set in filigree gold, which I kept in their own velvet-lined box.

He would hook out the box, rake it open, extract the earrings with his teeth and bat them around like marbles. I witnessed the whole procedure one night, sitting up in bed yelling at him to stop. He took no notice at all except to flatten his ears in reproof. Ladies didn't Shout, he said.

Annoyed – the earrings were good ones, doubly precious because they'd been given to me by Louisa – I started barricading the cupboard doors against him every night before I went to bed. Shoes against the jewellery cupboard, piled one on top of the other, one wedged under the bottom of the door. A scratching board, faced with carpet in reverse, sloped against the matching door, in the hope of distracting his attention. A large china storage jar marked SUGAR and filled with sand, against one of the doors of the cupboard that substituted for a tallboy. (Don't ask me why. I went berserk at that stage, gathering together anything I thought would deter him.)

It reminded me of the time when his predecessor, Saska, had started wetting on the rug in the hall and I'd had to cover it with a polythene sheet weighted down with heavy fire-irons, a portable heater and a crow-bar, and remove it all at top speed when anybody came up the front path. Only this was worse because Saphra was as skilful with his paws as Chinese juggler. Down would come the scratching board, whoosh would go the edges, open would fly the doors. Down would tumble the shoe pile, too, out would come the earring box and out would fall the earrings, and I'd leap out of bed, replace them, barricade the doors even more heavily and lie listening to the latest cat-burgling techniques being practised until he got tired and came to bed.

Why didn't I banish him downstairs to the sitting-room again? Because he wouldn't let Tani sleep when they were down there. Besides when they did go to sleep they looked such angels, so comforting curled together on the bed... Sometimes I woke in the morning and found that, Christmas-card picture or not, he'd been busy again while I slept. The earrings were out, the chain on the stairs, or a pair of tights lying mangled on the landing... and I'd hug him, forgive him, and put them all away again.

Then came the day when, cleaning the bedroom, I heard something rattle into the vacuum cleaner and decided I must have brought up a piece of gravel on the sole of my shoe. I went on vacuuming, spotted one of my earrings on the rug in front of the dressing-table, had a sudden dark suspicion as to where the other one might be... I bent down, examined the vacuum cleaner and my suspicion was confirmed. Out, when I lifted the cleaner, tumbled an oval jade stone minus its setting – which fell out after it in a jumble of mangled gold. I sat on the floor and wept, attended by two puzzled cats – one pale, paws folded precisely, assuring me as usual that Nothing was anything to do with her, she was a Good Girl; the other dark-masked, his almond eyes shining like sapphires, asking innocently what all the fuss was about. It was only a little green stone and I had another one.

I got the earring repaired. After my years of living with Siamese cats I was an expert at mending things myself, or tracking down somebody who could. My cousin Dee happened to be going to jewellery classes at the time. Her tutor was a craftsman jeweller, and he repaired the earring as if it had never been damaged. It cost a pretty penny, of course, and what he thought when he heard a cat had done it is anybody's guess, but I put it down to experience, transferred the earrings to the cupboard above the wardrobe, and girded myself once more to face the fray.

So passed the summer, with Saphra continually in trouble. I wouldn't have changed him for worlds, but the affairs of the village passed me by more or less at a distance. Certainly with very little impact. The Friendly Hands Club came back from their holiday jaunt, Mrs Binney not yet having officially landed her catch, though the general opinion of those who'd accompanied them was that it couldn't be very long now. Except, that was, for Fred Ferry's father Sam, who'd gone along the trip himself, arthritis and all, and whose comment was that that Tooting bloke was an adjectival twit and if Maude married he so was she.

It seemed that Mr Tooting had tried to show Sam how best to mount the steps to a museum with the aid of his stick. Sam, having a temper like his son's – and more sense, he'd informed his would-be mentor, than any ruddy townie wearin' a piddlin' pig-keeper's hat – had poked Mr Tooting in the knee with the stick to move him out of the way, Mr Tooting had fallen down the steps, and the coach party had had its biggest laugh of the holiday. The two were not now speaking to each other, and another village feud was in existence.

Nearer home, Poppy Richards had moved into her cottage and was busy settling in and interesting herself in local affairs. She seemed much more sensible than her sister, from what I'd seen of her. She liked Saphra and stopped to talk to him when she went by, and had been added to his list of friends.

Still nearer home, down the lane past Father Adams, Janet and Peter Reason had added four geese and half a dozen ducks to the two horses, labrador dog and tabby cat they already owned, and things had livened up no end. The Reasons had a considerable amount of land, spreading up towards me in one direction and almost the whole of the rest of the way down the valley in the other. The lane, a rough-surfaced bridletrack, ran through the middle of it, fenced only where it passed the horses' field, and for the rest of its length open to the Reasons' low cottage terrace on the right-hand side and their large parking area and stretch of woodland on the other. A wonderful place for a swashbuckling gander and his entourage to wander abroad in, and wander and swashbuckle they did.

Almost any hour of the day except after lunch, when they took a siesta on the sloping lawn above the terrace, Gerald the gander and his wives could be seen marching up the lane, down the hill, or past my side gate and up the forestry track, swaying from side to side like a quartet of outsize skittles, honking to let the world know they were coming and followed, like children trailing a Salvation Army band, by a huddle of quacking ducks.

They ventured incredible distances – far up the lane beyond me, stopping to look in at the gateways of the two other cottages along the route and honk defiance at the Alsatian which thrust its head through a cat-flap in the door of one of them and barked; way up the hill to the farm where they would peer patronisingly in at the unenterprising farm geese in their paddock; on to the Rose and Crown on the corner, before turning, and parading slowly back. Always with Gerald in front like a standard-bearer and the ducks bringing up the rear. And, as the weeks went by and nobody opposed him, with Gerald growing more belligerent.

He offered to fight Fred Ferry whenever they met on the hill. Fred, being a countryman and used to geese, merely swung his knapsack to fend him off and said 'Why dussn't thee go and pester Old Pans?' (Old Pans, incidentally, wasn't nearly as dim as Fred thought she was. When Gerald passed she was usually inside her gate with the bolt on, throwing bread across to land outside Fred's.) Any time walkers ventured down the lane to Gerald's own cottage he stood in the middle of it and dared them, and the walkers usually turned back. Aided by his army, too, Gerald had a wonderful time every Friday morning, when the men from the Council came to check the swallet.

Our local swallet is in the stream bank further up in the forest, and when the stream swells after heavy rain the surplus water, in theory, goes down the swallet into underground caves and comes out, as has been proved by putting dye in it, in a village pond five miles away. If, however, the swallet is blocked by silt and stones brought down by the force of the water, the stream overflows its banks, rushes down like the Lynn in full spate, and washes away the lane surface.

To prevent this, once a week two hefty Council workers parked their van outside my cottage, strolled up to the swallet carrying spades, cleared it of any blockage, ambled back checking the ditch for debris and overhanging brambles, went on down to the Reasons' to check there was no obstruction where the stream crossed the bridleway into the horses' field, then ambled back for a cigarette and an appreciative breath of valley air before heading off back to base.

That was how it was before the coming of Gerald and his supporters. After that, the moment the Council van stopped outside, a procession would appear coming up the lane – a procession in a hurry this time: no time for honking – and when the men opened the van doors to get out they would find themselves confronted by four geese hissing away like steam jets against a backcloth of excited ducks. By dint of brandishing their spades the men would manage to get past them and up the lane to see to the swallet. It was when they returned that the real fun would start. As they passed the van and started down the Reasons' lane, the geese would emerge from behind my coal-shed, where they'd been waiting, and close in behind them. Hissing, rattling their big orange bills, feinting with outstretched necks at the men's legs and having a whale of a time.

One of the men was pretty good at avoiding them. The other, a big bearded man a good six feet tall, was scared stiff and usually ended up doing a sort of jig on the spot, surrounded by geese and ducks and yelling for help. When that happened, if Janet was home she would come to his rescue. If she'd gone to work then I'd go out, wave my crook at them and the geese would disperse. Laughing their heads off by the look of them. I never heard of them actually hurting anybody. And, as Janet said, she couldn't keep them shut in. She was away all day; they were there to eat down the grass;

and eat the grass – and police the valley – they did most successfully.

It was mostly the Council men they intimidated, but occasionally they had a go at me. Sometimes, if I was going to town, I would reverse the car out of the garage and park it in front of the cottage before I changed out of my jeans. Up would hurry the geese, ready for their favourite sport, and I would have to open an umbrella at them before I could get out. I kept a red umbrella ready on the passenger seat, and the sight of me backing behind it like a matador towards the safety of my front gate intrigued many a visitor to the valley. Visitors in cars, that was. Nobody would have ventured out on foot.

If I was in the garden with the cats when the geese went by, Tani would bolt, stomach to the ground, into the cottage and hide under the sofa while Saphra, who was made of stronger stuff, watched from the garden wall. Protected by the stream which ran beneath him like a moat he would crouch, wailing defiance at them. He wasn't Afraid. He'd take on the Lot of Them. Just let them Try Anything, he'd howl, with a quick look over his shoulder to make sure I was at back-up position behind him.

It took more than a Siamese cat to put Gerald and Co. in their place, however. Way down past Father Adams's, who surprisingly had no trouble with the geese himself (maybe Gerald knew better than to chance his luck with a real countryman), Peter Reason had constructed a pond for them at the side of the lane by damming the stream, and it so happened that my cousin Dee came out to tea one day, bringing her border terrier Tilly and her friend's cross-Bedlington bitch Tag, whom she was looking after while her friend was on holiday.

We had tea on the lawn with the cats in their run for safety, bees humming in the lavender behind us, white summer clouds drifting like sailing ships over the grass-grown ramparts of the Iron Age fort on the hill at the end of the valley and a buzzard hovering silently overhead. 'No wonder you love it here,' sighed Dee relaxing in her chair. 'I can't think of any place on earth more peaceful.'

She didn't say that half an hour later, when we went out to put the dogs in the car. Tilly, who'd been spayed the previous week and was being rather careful how she moved, stood by the car door waiting to get in. Tag, milling about at the edge of the stream, was sniffing the various scents, when she suddenly heard something down the lane. Her head came up, she saw big white wings flapping like tablecloths down at the pond, and she was gone like an arrow.

'Tag!' Dee and I shrieked in terrified unison. 'Tag! Come back!' She dashed into the mêlée of geese, scattering them in all directions, and then, like the obedient dog she was, she did come back, trotting up the lane with her tongue lolling happily at the fun she'd had. Unfortunately she'd set the stage for melodrama. Roused by the hullabaloo Tilly, forgetting her stitches, tore down the lane, passed Tag without a glance, and jumped on the nearest goose, which immediately sank beneath the pond surface with Tilly on her back and stayed there.

'Tilly!' we yelled, starting to run ourselves. As we reached the pond Tilly fell off into the water, scrambled ashore, and the goose popped up as if on water wings. Unfortunately not for long. Tilly jumped on her again, they went down like a submarine and its conning tower, and while we were still trying to get a grip on Tilly Janet came racing up from the stables, jumped into the pond, grabbed Tilly by her collar and threw her ashore. Up came the goose again, and beat it hastily for the opposite shore, where Gerald and the others were honking in circles.

Wading out of the pond, Janet dealt Tilly a well-deserved slap. Dee, cuddling the miscreant in her arms, turned her back to shield her. 'Don't hurt her. She's just had a hysterectomy,' she wailed.

'She should know better,' snapped Janet angrily. And we couldn't flaw that one. So she jolly well should.

All the way up the lane Dee agonised as to what she should do. Go back and apologise to Janet? I'd do that, I said. Better for Dee to take the dogs home out of the way before anything else happened. Offer to pay damages? I'd pass the message on, I said. Though I really didn't think there'd be any.

Dee safely away with the dogs – and was I glad to see the back of them – I went down the lane to see Janet. There was no sign of the geese. Only, over in a corner of the field by a ruined shed, something big and round and white lay half-concealed in a clump of nettles. Surely the goose hadn't died of shock? How on earth was I going to tell Janet? Coward-like, I didn't. Just apologised and asked how they were. I'd check on the way back, and if there was a defunct goose there I'd decide how to break the news to the Reasons later.

Janet received me just as worriedly. The geese were all right, she assured me (she didn't know about that big white bottom up the lane). She was sorry, though, that she'd slapped Tilly. She'd done it in the heat of the moment. Tilly had deserved it, I said. I must ring Dee, though, and tell her to bath Tilly in a Dettol solution, Janet insisted. With a half-healed incision... one never knew what germs there were in duck-ponds. I promised that I would, came relievedly up the lane – especially when I'd looked more closely at the round white thing in the nettles and found it wasn't a dead goose only an old white enamelled bowl thrown there by some long-gone valley resident in the days before refuse collections – and went up to get the cats in for their supper.

He wished he could have played with those dogs, said Saphra, who'd been sitting watching the whole thing in the cat-run. They knew how to have fun.

Hadn't realised they were white slaver dogs, had he? observed Tani, emerging from the cat-house with the alacrity which was her wont when visitors had gone. It was a good thing she had Brains enough for Both of them.

he did, one paw on the end of it, as he'd seen me use my hand, then rushing round to the front to see whether the mouse had appeared. Sometimes it had, and Saph was overjoyed, tossing it in the air in triumph before pushing it back to do the wiggling bit again. More often than not it hadn't, because he was wiggling the ruler blindly – but he'd reasoned out the connection and worked at it like an engineer manipulating a lever.

One of the most remarkable instances of this sort I've heard was told me by a breeder who'd sold a kitten to some people who'd never experienced the proclivities of Siamese before and kept ringing her to tell her what he'd been up to. It seemed that they'd been having their house re-wired and the kitten kept going under the floorboards and coming out somewhere else. They did their best to stop him, but given the chance he was underground like a flash, and it took ages of expensive working time to get him out. Then the electrician hit on the idea of tying a length of string to the kitten's collar, putting him under the floorboards, calling him from across the room where they'd taken up another board, and the kitten would nip across underneath, emerge gleefully from the new hole – and the electrician would tie the string to a length of flex which he then pulled through and connected up. 'Saved hours of taking up floorboards,' said the breeder proudly. I would have been scared of the string's getting caught round a joist and their having to take up floorboards even faster than before to get the kitten out, but maybe he was an exception. Maybe he's working even now as an electrician's mate. I never heard the sequel. Only wondered, thinking of Saphra using the carpenter's ruler as an extension of his arm, what one might have made of him with a little encouragement.

I hear lots of stories about intelligent cats. Not always Siamese. All breeds, including 'ordinaries', have their A-level types. There was the tale I heard from a chemist in a neighbouring village, whose enormous, battlescarred ginger neuter suddenly took to staying out for hours at a time and then coming home smelling of Chanel No.5, which the chemist recognised because he sold it in his shop. Intrigued, one day he followed the cat, which walked a long way up the road, scorning the lesser houses, and finally turned in at the gateway of the local 'big house', proceeding up the drive as if he owned it. He went to the front door, lifted the low-level letter-box with his nose and let it drop. Within seconds the door opened, a voice said 'There you are darling, come right in' and the cat disappeared inside – to reappear at his home several hours later smelling once more of Chanel No.5. The chemist said a wealthy old lady lived in the big house and was obviously feeding and making a fuss of him, hence the smell of the expensive scent, which the cat apparently didn't mind. 'Yet he looks like a prize-fighter,' he said incredulously.

The same cat, more in keeping with its appearance, once ate all the fish in the chemist's friend's garden pond. The friend, who also lived a long way up the same road, said he couldn't understand why his fish were vanishing. 'Perhaps a heron's taking them,' suggested the chemist, who had no idea of the truth – until one day he met his cat walking down the middle of the road with the last – and largest – goldfish in its mouth, tail flapping on one side, head wagging on the other. The chemist tried to rescue it, but the cat wouldn't let go, so he had to carry the cat home, fish and all, as fast as he could, before anybody could see them. Next time he met the fish-owner the man said he was re-stocking the pond with small ones. Presumably they were beneath the cat's notice, as he never took any again. 'Can you beat that?' asked the chemist. I had to admit that I couldn't.

Neither could I beat the story about somebody, living in the country with two cocker spaniels, who in an unguarded moment adopted a black half-Siamese kitten from a friend who lived in town. On arrival the kitten stalked into the kitchen, put the spaniels in their places by slapping them on the nose, and took to country life straight away. The following day his new owner heard puffing and snorting coming from an adjoining field and found the kitten smacking the nose of a cow which was standing over him looking threatening. The cow was likewise put in its place. Later, while his owner watched in horror, the kitten leapt on to the back of a bullock, clung to the curls on its neck, and hung on like a rodeo rider while it careered round the field. Encouraged by his success, he was next found sitting behind a cow batting happily at her tail, which the cow, presumably thinking an outsize fly was after her, was swishing angrily from side to side. On another occasion he stalked a magpie, grabbed a tail-feather as it took off, and was airborne until the feather came away. Picking himself up, the kitten took the feather indoors and it was a treasure for days until it became too dilapidated to play with or take to bed. And when he wasn't dicing with death, finished his owner, he liked to sit in a holly tree by the front door eating the leaves and removing the prickles from his mouth with his paw. What did I make of that? I could only say, weakly, 'It must be the Siamese in him.'

Half-Siamese resulting from unplanned matings with domestic cats, typified by their elegant lines, plush coats and foghorn voices, are often black and invariably more catastrophe-prone than ordinary cats. The modern pedigreed Orientals which are the result of deliberate crossings between Siamese and other selected cats also have this reputation, but I find it hard to believe, after my own experience and all the hair-raising tales I've heard, that there is anything to beat a full Siamese for causing trouble. Consider the story I was told by the woman who took her Siamese kitten – the first she'd ever had, and she was captivated by the way it accompanied her everywhere like a dog – to a house a couple of streets away to buy potatoes from an old man who sold vegetables to supplement his pension. Frightened by the traffic, which it hadn't experienced before, as soon as the man opened the door the kitten ran up his leg. 'His bad leg, of course,' said my informant resignedly.

She peeled the protesting Alfred off the old man's back and took him home, and the next time she went round for potatoes – without Alfred for obvious reasons – she was duly shown the wounds on the door-step. Up went the old man's trouser leg. 'See where 'e got I? Cor, I felt that. Hummin' all night it were,' he informed her. Not that she could see anything. She was too busy praying that nobody spotted the display and reported them for indecent exposure.

'The number of people who say what a beautiful cat he is and then spoil it by saying they knew he must be mine...' she finished.

I am continually hearing stories like this, though there are people who insist I make it all up and that no cats could ever behave as I say Siamese do. They are non-Siamese owners, of course, and I can only suggest they try it for themselves – like the woman who rang me one day about her chocolate-point Siamese, the first she'd ever owned, wondering if I could help her.

I shuddered the moment I heard his name. In my experience, to call a Siamese Ming, as being the epitome of Oriental fragility and perfection, is courting disaster. All the Mings I've ever come across have been outstandingly diabolical as if their one mission in life is to disprove the connotation, and this Ming was no exception.

His owner, Connie, explained that she had recently retired from teaching science at a girls' boarding school and had moved into a new flat. The garden of her previous flat had opened on to a large field in which it had been safe for Ming to roam while she was away, and there he'd set up his personal dictatorship. He'd fought all the other neighbourhood cats – in particular one called Ginger Bates, whom he'd loathed with deep Oriental loathing. He'd stolen things from the neighbours and brought them home to her as gifts and she'd had to find out whom they belonged to and return them. He'd walked the world like a feline Dick Turpin and now that his owner had brought him to a flat more convenient for her – near the first one but round the corner on the main road, with the garden wired in for his safety and Ginger

Bates and his beloved field on the other side of an eight-foot fence – he'd embarked on despotic revolution.

He'd always been a despot, his owner informed me. He'd originally belonged to her vet who had two other Siamese whom Ming, as a youngster, had bullied till their lives weren't worth living – and, as she was catless at the time, the vet and his wife, who were friends of hers, had asked her to take him on.

He'd settled well with Connie. He liked electric fires, and prawns and steak, and being treated as an only cat of special importance. But he disapproved strongly of the new flat when they moved, and particularly of the wired-in garden. They'd been in residence for three weeks, during which time he'd patrolled the bottom of the fence every day, clawing at the wooden supports, yelling because he couldn't get over or under it, and her new neighbours had started to complain. What could she *do*, short of finding another flat and moving away? she asked. She couldn't part with Ming. He was her friend.

Get a water-pistol, I advised her, explaining how it had worked with Saphra. I could sense horror coming down the phone wire at the suggestion. What about a flower spray? she asked at last. I understood her predicament. She lived very near the school where she had taught, and still took part in its extracurricular activities. An ex-senior mistress going round with a water-pistol – or spotted in the local toy shop trying to buy one – would hardly set a good example to the pupils.

Try the flower spray then, I agreed. But she must *persevere*, not give up on it. The vet had told her to persevere, too, she admitted dismally. It hadn't worked with him, though, when he'd owned Ming in the beginning.

It worked this time. Three weeks later Connie was on the phone again. She didn't know how to thank me, she said. Ming had given up bawling and accepted the fact that he couldn't get out, though he still peered under the fence for Ginger Bates. So far the latter hadn't peered back, for which she was truly grateful. Ming already had a permanently crumpled ear as the result of an encounter with a magpie whose nest he'd tried to raid in the old free-roaming field days, and she had always been afraid of his getting another from Ginger Bates.

She gave me a résumé of Ming's eventful history – of his many fights and consequent visits to the vet. He also suffered frequently from tonsillitis on account of talking so much, and had to be treated for that, which was no picnic. The things he'd stolen and brought home to the previous flat to await her return from school, she expounded earnestly, ranged from fillets of steak and a turbot skeleton with its head on to green balls lifted from the public tennis courts when nobody was looking, and parked one on each stair. How he'd carried them home she couldn't imagine, but he had. And only green ones.

As far as she could she'd tracked down the owners and returned the booty, but sometimes it had been impossible – for instance when she got home and found two pairs of red knickers laid out on the stairs with Ming sitting beside them saying they were a Present. She couldn't go round asking about those, she said: it would have been too embarrassing. She'd put them in the dustbin, but it had always remained on her conscience. Why did Siamese cats do such awful things?

I roared with laughter. Because they were Siamese, I said. And from what she'd told me I wouldn't mind betting, if we compared pedigrees, that he and Saphra were related. Saphra did things like that because he'd got his character from his grandfather, Saturn Sentinel, of the famous Killdown strain. People were fortunate, or benighted, depending on how one looked at it, if they had one of that line. Life was never the same again. I told her about Saphra and the purple towels and his being expelled from Langford. It was her turn to shudder down the phone.

By the next post she sent me a copy of Ming's pedigree and sure enough, there it was. Saturn Sentinel was Ming's grandfather, he and Saph were cousins. It didn't matter how far they were removed from their illustrious ancestor, I told her when I rang to break the news. If the genes were there, she was in for trouble.

We became friends – comrades in distress – at the very thought of it. She came to see my two – Saphra the extrovert Head of the Household, Tani pursuing her role of Fugitive from the White Slavers as usual – and was entranced by them. I went to see Ming, and was immediately captivated by him. Chocolate-pointed – a paler edition of Saphra – he was very like Saph, except for the crumpled ear. Handsome, tall – impressively so when he put on his Collapsing with the Cold performance, which was one of the first things he tried out on me.

Connie's flat had gas-fired central heating, with a large electric fire in the sitting-room to boost the temperature when necessary. It was November when I first went to visit her, and I'd met Ming, we'd had tea and were relaxing in the sitting-room when I happened to glance to my left, where there was a long radiator under the window. There, sitting upright, stretched to his full height against it with his head pressed wanly against the metalwork and his eyes closed was Ming. I bent down to look at him. He half-opened one eye, saw me watching him and leaned more heavily still against the radiator. I got the message. He was Suffering. Feeling the Cold. 'Any minute now you'll get the fire routine,' muttered Connie under her breath. A moment later I did. He walked over the electric fire, sat down in front of it and batted the plug, which was lying loose, till it rattled against the wall. 'WOW!' he said with feeling, fixing me with a look.

To illustrate what he expected to happen next, Connie put the plug in the socket and switched on the fire. As the heat came up and the element began to glow, Ming stretched himself in front of it and rolled on his back. Bliss! said his expression. If he could put the plug in the socket himself he would, said Connie. Any day now she expected him to work out how to do it.

He'd already worked out one thing that was quite extraordinary. Indeed, it was the most remarkable example of cat intelligence I've ever come across. There was a cat-flap in the kitchen door leading into the fenced-in garden, to which Ming usually had unrestricted access. When Connie was going to be out, however, she brought Ming indoors, put the fastener down on the cat-flap and a small but weighty cupboard in front of the flap. She was afraid that, with plenty of time and no supervision, he might still find a way to scale the fence.

Connie, who is one of the country's experts on wild orchids, would from time to time be away overnight giving a lecture or visiting other botanists, and her friend Diana would take charge of Ming. Di, who ran her own car-transport business, had flexible hours and would come in to keep Ming company during the day. She would feed him and let him out into the garden, and bring him in and secure the cat-flap when she was leaving. An added twist to this routine was that he greeted Di with affection when she came to be company to him, butting her with his head, winding himself round her legs, lying against her neck and purring when she picked him up.

When Connie returned from wherever she'd been however, and Di fetched her from the station and the two of them went into the house, Ming would hide under the bed, cringing away from Di and wailing up and down the scale about how much she frightened him and he hated her – a put-on act to make Connie think his life was intolerable while she was away which might have worked, so accomplished an actor was he, if Di hadn't persuaded Connie to stay hidden outside one day while she, Di, went into the house alone. With her own eyes Connie saw that cat, through the kitchen window, rubbing his face abandonedly against Di's, cupboard-loving with all his might – till Connie put in an appearance and he jumped from Di's arms, spitting blue murder at her, and fled.

That is by the way. The real story concerns the occasion when Di, having been with Ming during the early evening, and brought him in from the garden and fastened the cat-flap, went in later to give him a meal and a cuddle before his bedtime, only to find Ming missing, an open cat-flap in the kitchen with the cupboard moved aside from it, and deep black night outside.

Di's first thought was that she must have left the cat-flap unfastened and omitted to put the cupboard in front of it. Yet she was sure she'd taken both precautions. The question was where was Ming now? She went into the garden with a torch, shone it around, scarcely daring to breathe in case he'd somehow managed to get over the fence – and there he was. It was the frog season and he was sitting frog-watching in the border. She brought him in, fastened the cat-flap and barricaded it once more, and when Connie returned told her just what had happened.

Next day, determined to find out how he'd done it, Connie seated herself in the spare room from which, with the doors open, she had a clear view across the hall and through the kitchen to the barricaded flap. After a while Ming emerged from her bedroom, where he'd been napping on the bed, made his way to the kitchen and seated himself in front of the cupboard, prising the door open after a few minutes' activity with a hooked left claw. That done, he inserted his right paw in the open front of the small cupboard, put it behind the cupboard door and pulled. Slightly to the left, so that the cupboard slid sideways away from the cat-flap, on which he then undid the fastener to let himself through.

Any time Connie went out after that she reinforced the cupboard by setting the kitchen table against it, and jamming the kitchen chairs tightly against that. So far Ming hadn't solved the problem of moving that lot but he was probably working on it, said Connie, and it looked awful when she had people staying.

When Saphra left home to prove he was a Killdown (or was it the adventure stories Sinbad had told him?) he didn't bother about cat-flaps. For safety's sake there wasn't one in the back door anyway, and he did it the way he'd always planned: by hiding in his lair behind the freezer when I was changing the litter trays and hoping I wouldn't shut the door properly. One day his luck was in: I didn't. I kicked it behind me and it hadn't clicked.

By the time I discovered it he must have been gone some time. I scoured the garden, ran up and down the lane rattling the cat-biscuit tin and calling. There was no sign. All was silence. Tani, when I asked her where he was, said she hadn't seen him. White Slavers had probably got him, she said.

I was standing at the gate, wondering which way, to turn next, when I saw a procession coming up the lane. A crowd of walkers – dozens of them, all wearing psychedelically-coloured rucksacks, following behind a leader who was carrying a cat in his arms. I'd seen them through the window earlier, going in the opposite direction. They hadn't had a cat with them then. I knew immediately who it was.

It had followed them, said the leader. Its movements had been noted by various members of the group. One had seen it on the wall, craning its neck at the rucksacks.

Another had seen it jump down and start following them. Several had tried to shoo it back, but it had taken no notice. Just dodged them and kept on going, they said. It wasn't till they reached the bottom lane and started to climb the steep hillside up to the ancient camp that they realised Saphra wasn't just taking a cattish stroll. He was deliberately accompanying them. They were on their way to Burrington, to see the Rock of Ages. Miles across the hills, and they weren't coming back in this direction. So they thought they'd better bring him back – all of them together, because it was an organised party which wouldn't have known its way without the leader.

I thanked them and held him while they started off once more. He was indignant, and would have followed them again if I'd let him. He was Stupid, said Tani. Of course they'd brought him back. They knew he wasn't a Proper Walker. They wouldn't have known if he'd been wearing a rucksack, said Saphra who, like all Siamese, thought of himself as a human being. It was worrying all the same. Some weeks earlier Janet's cat, down the lane, had gone missing. It was found, after a fortnight, right on top of Mendip, sheltering under a fallen tree and practically starving. It, too, was thought to have followed a walking party – one not so caring as the group that brought back Saphra.

I was still worrying about it – how quickly it had happened; the need to watch his every movement, and see that the back door was closed – when, that afternoon, across in the woods getting logs and carrying the electric chainsaw, I caught my foot in a bramble and went flying. I rolled down the hillside, ripped my knee on the thorns so that it looked as though I'd been mauled by an angry lion and ended up, my knee patched with sticking plaster, flat on my back on the sitting-room floor attempting to compose myself with relaxation. I had my eyes closed, trying to blank out the tensions of the day, when I suddenly sensed that I wasn't alone. I opened my eyes. Sure enough, I wasn't. Seated side by side at my feet like a pair of candles at a catafalque, staring at me intently, were Tani and Saphra. It was past six o'clock – time for their meal – and they were willing me to remember it. I got up at once. Siamese owners know their place, even when they're at the end of their tether.

The day wasn't over yet. Still limping round and feeling sorry for myself, that very evening I was called out to what looked like rivalling the mystery of the Marie Celeste. Miss Wellington had come down to the valley on one of her nocturnal rambles – to check that the stream was running properly, she said – and had decided to call on her sister. She'd climbed up the side lane to Poppy's cottage, knocked on the door and, getting no answer, lifted the latch and let herself in. She found an ironing board set up in the kitchen, a half-ironed blouse on it (the flatiron had been switched off, which itself added to the mystery) – but, though she had searched, heart in mouth, through every room in the cottage, there had been absolutely no sign of Poppy.

I limped womanfully back with her. Searched every room myself. Looked in the garage. Her car, even more confoundingly, was still there. Poppy, Miss W. decided, must have been kidnapped, though for what reason, since she was neither young and beautiful nor wealthy, I couldn't imagine. She hadn't been going anywhere that night, wept Miss W. She'd have told her if she had been. We were on the point of calling the police – I'd been deputed to dial 999 – when, as I raised the receiver, I heard a car door slam in the lane outside, Poppy's voice wishing someone goodnight, and in she came. Safe, if a trifle flushed. At seeing us there, it struck me.

The explanation was simple when we heard it. Poppy, since her arrival in the village, had joined many of the local activities and, being an ex-headmistress and used to authority, had rapidly wafted to the forefront of several of them. Among other things she was on the committee of the Friendly Hands Club and a committee meeting had been fixed for that night – something she'd quite forgotten, having already been to the library committee meeting in the afternoon. When she didn't turn up at the village hall at eight o'clock, and there was no nearby phone on which they could contact her, Mr Tooting, who had also come from another meeting and had brought his car, volunteered to drive over to find out what had delayed her.

Surprised in the middle of her ironing, appalled at having made such a mistake, Poppy had switched off the iron, put on her coat and gone with him at once. She hadn't thought to phone her sister – it had all been such a frantic rush anyway. All this she explained to Miss Wellington, who was only too relieved to find her intact. One heard such awful things nowadays, said Miss W. And how kind of Mr Tooting to bring her back afterwards. It was indeed. There was only one thing. That flush on Poppy's face. It made me wonder.

TWELVE

It made Mrs Binney wonder, too. The news that Poppy Richards had been seen riding in Mr Tooting's car reached her practically at the speed of sound. Fred Ferry saw them going past the Rose and Crown; he told his father who lived two doors away from Mrs B, and Sam Ferry, in pursuance of the feud that had started on the Friendly Hands holiday, made it his business to pass it on to her the same evening.

Sam, also as a result of the feud, had taken to dressing much more smartly of late. Where he would once upon a time have gone along to the pub in his shirt-sleeves for his mid-day pint and stayed like that for the rest of the day, he now wore smartly pressed trousers, collar and tie and a mustard and brown checked jacket when he went out – presumably to show he was as good as Mr Tooting, though he stopped short of wearing a pork-pie hat. Sam's wiry thatch reared itself around the village as rampant as, and forcefully remindful of, an outsize shaving brush – which was more, I gathered from Mrs Adams, than could be said when Mr Tooting took his hat off at the Social Club. Sam, in fact, was looking a sight more presentable than his son Fred these days. Even the walking stick necessitated by his arthritis didn't detract from the image. If anything it added a touch of elder-statesman distinction that must have had an effect on Mrs Binney because she came down next day to tell me what Sam had said and to find out, by circuitous questioning, what I knew about the matter. I allayed her suspicions by telling her about the forgotten committee meeting and she said, with a superior sniff, 'Some people takes on more than they can manage just for the show of it,' and started back up the hill obviously mollified by what she'd heard.

Hardly had she left when I had another visitor leaning on the gate – this time Will Woodrow, an elderly retired farmer from over the hill who occasionally walked down through the valley with his old dog and, if I was about, liked to stop and reminisce about the countryside in his young days, knowing I always enjoyed his stories.

'Thass Maude Binney, innit? Maude Miles as was?' he said, peering interestedly up the hillside after her. Mrs Binney, flaunting her violet curls and wearing an emerald green autumn coat obviously chosen with the help of Shirl, looked more like a hyacinth than ever, and to old Mr Woodrow she was evidently well worth peering after.

'Han't seen she in years,' he remarked. 'Wears purty well, don't she? Might call on her one day and see how she's doin'.' There was a gleam in his eye as he said it. Mr Woodrow was himself a widower.

'D'ust remember her uncle, old Walt Miles?' he went on. I said firmly that he was before my time in the village. 'Ah,' he nodded. 'Suppose he would be. But he were a card, I can tell thee. Used to be odd-job man at Downton Farm, up t'other end of the valley, back in the days when workin' men wore bowler hats and red hankerchers round their necks. He were a good worker and Farmer thought a lot of 'n – but there come a time when pats of butter started disappearin' from the dairy, and Farmer were sure that Walt were takin' 'em. He didn't want to upset th'apple cart by tacklin' 'n about it straight out, though, so he and his wife put their heads together and one day they invited 'n in for a glass of cider. They sat 'n on the settle in front of the fire, which they'd stoked up high. Walt always kept his bowler on, whatever he were doin', and he did then too, in spite of their invitin' 'n to take it off. After a bit, sure enough, butter started to run down his face. Walt mopped it with his red hankercher. It went on runnin'. Farmer and his wife took no notice – just went on talkin' as if nuthin' had happened. In th'end Walt excused hisself and near fell over the settle gettin' to the door, his face swimmin' in butter. Nobody said a word about it – but no butter pats ever went missin' after that.'

I laughed a lot about Uncle Walt and, encouraged, Mr Woodrow started off again.

'They bowlers was handy for a lot of things,' he said. 'There were another fellow – old George Thorn – who used to do the same sort of job over at Tiptree. Then one day, when he was supposed to be workin' in the yard, the farmer noticed 'n disappearin' over the wall. Farmer wondered what he were up to, so he crept up and looked over to see. George had his bowler on the ground and was crouchin' in front of a gleanie's' – guinea-fowl's – 'nest he must have spotted there, and he was ladling out the eggs. "One for Master," he counted (he left he in the nest). "One for I." (He put he in his bowler.) "One for Master..." he went on till there was only one left. And as he was lookin' at that 'un and hesitatin', Farmer put his hand over the wall and took it hisself. "Reckon Master had better have he," he said.'

I laughed appreciatively again and Mr Woodrow, well into his stride by now, asked if I remembered the old Rector's wife – 'she what had one of they peakyneeses'. I said I did. She and her husband were in charge of the parish when Charles and I first came to the valley. 'Bit of an old flanneller,' observed Mr Woodrow. 'Always soapin' people up.' She was only trying to be friendly, I protested. I'd always had a soft spot for the old girl. She'd been very kind to me.

'Thass as maybe,' he said. 'Anyway, there was these two men what cleared an old overgrown garden round a ruined cottage in the village and planted it with vegetables – sort of an allotment, like, to help out their own. 'N one day one of 'em was liftin' taters there when along comes Rector's wife with her dog, and she looks over the wall and says "You and the Lord have made a good job of that, Albert." "Dunno about that," says Albert. "Lord had this lot to hisself for a hell of a time, and he din't get much done on his own."'

With which, and a wicked grin, Mr Woodrow touched the brim of his battered old trilby, called his dog and plodded on past the gate. Not down the lane in the direction of the Reasons' cottage, which was his usual route, but up the hill in the wake of Mrs Binney. Interesting, but I hadn't the time that autumn to follow up the convolutions of village affairs. The inside of the cottage badly needed redecorating and, as I'd been warned never to let Bill the ambulance man do anything indoors, I was busy doing the job myself.

I started with the sitting-room. It being the only living room, I couldn't empty it and give up several days to the work. I had to do it a wall at a time, taking down the pictures, and the books from the bookshelves, moving the furniture so I could get behind it, and at the end of the day, when the paint was dry, putting it all back in place again. It was wet outside, too, and turning cold – not the sort of weather for Tani and Saphra to be out in their house – so I had a big log fire going in the fireplace to dry the walls as I worked, with the Snoozabed in front of it for the cats to sit on.

Only they didn't. I had dust sheets over the furniture and the stacked-up piles of books, and the cats spent most of their time underneath them. Leaping about, wiggling their paws through gaps trying to get me to play with them – they thought it was a game put on for their amusement. As fast as I threw a sheet over a chair there would be a rush and a dive and two cats would be squirming about underneath it. Tani knocked over brushes, Saphra got paint on himself – emulsion paint, fortunately, which I could get off with water. Oil-based paints have to be removed with spirit, and turps or white spirit are lethal to cats. I had often worried about what to do if a cat did get gloss or undercoat on itself, and a reader writing to me about the misdeeds of her Siamese supplied the answer. Wipe the paint off with gin or vodka, she said. That would do the trick. She kept a bottle of gin in the paint cupboard specially for use on her cat, Tao, who was always getting paint on himself. Sometimes she thought he did it purposely in order to be rubbed with his favourite tipple – and if visitors looked askance at times and sniffed the air... it was part of the price one paid, she said, to live with a Siamese cat.

Saph had never tasted gin, but he did like whisky and sherry: he turned after his uncle Saska in that. It was bad enough when I had guests and he used to sit in front of them willing them to give him licks off their fingers, but giving him a taste for gin or vodka and letting him associate it with getting paint on himself – that would have been asking for trouble. He'd have been stuck to every newly painted door in the place. So, rainy weather or not, on glossing days he and Tani were banished to their garden house with the heater on.

The sitting-room was finished and, encouraged by the result, I decided to get a new carpet. It is a large room and the cost, I knew, would be prohibitive in the ordinary way. So one day I drove down to the Wilton carpet factory near Salisbury and found in their factory shop, just what I was looking for. A hardwearing apple-green broadloom carpet in two sections that would just fit my L-shaped room and which, with a bit of luck, I could lay myself. It would have cost a lot to have it delivered to Somerset, so I had them pack one section into the car boot and the other on to the back seat and got my neighbours to help me unload it into the garage when I got home. There it lay along one side, on top of a stack of ladders, and when Bill the ambulance man rang the next night to say he'd be coming at the weekend to start digging the earth from the back of the cottage – it had slipped down from the hillside over the years, and was blocking the path behind and causing dampness in the kitchen – I told him about the carpet and said I'd like him, when he did come, to help me carry it down to the cottage: it was too heavy for me to manage on my own.

I should have known better, of course. Ten minutes later Bill, having said yes, he'd help with the carpet at the weekend, came belting down the hill in his car. 'Thought you might like it right away,' he said. 'Then you can get on with putting it down.'

'It's raining,' I said aghast. 'It'll drag along the ground and get muddy. I can't lift it very high because of my back.' I had arthritis in it – the result, my doctor told me blithely, of doing so much riding in the past. And they tell you to take plenty of exercise...

He'd carry it, Bill assured me. He'd take the weight in the middle. I need only hold the front end lightly, to guide it.

You can guess what happened. The rolls were longer than he thought and, held in the middle, they sagged. I supported them in front, he held the middle, and the back ends dragged drearily, unnoticed till we reached the cottage, down the rain-sogged path. I suggested sliding them in through one of the sitting-room windows, to avoid turning a corner with them if we brought them through the hall, and that was another mistake. Bill slid each one over the window frame, came in and pulled them through the rest of the way himself to save me having to haul on them, stacked them one on top of the other along the wall beneath the window, dusted his hands at having accomplished his mission – and I let out a wail.

'Look at my fresh paint,' I moaned. It wasn't any more. Where the muddied carpet had brushed against the wall there were long black gritty steaks, like a Plimsollline along the side of a ship.

'That'll wash off,' said Bill complacently, and away he went, glowing with virtue at a good deed well done, leaving me to clean the wall as best I could and try to protect the carpet from the attentions of the two cats who, when eventually let into the room, discovered what they took to be the biggest stropping post in the world laid out along the wall especially for their benefit. It was the hessian backing that was the attraction – specially geared to their claws. They stropped away on it all the evening, daring each other with raised backs, bushing their tails, dashing up and down the length of the roll. It was obvious it was going to have to be laid as quickly as possible If I was to have a carpet left at all, so I rang Dora and Nita who had volunteered to help me put it down after the weekend, asking whether they could come the next day instead. They couldn't. They had an engagement they couldn't alter. Not to worry, I'd put it down by myself, I said, more airily than I felt.

The next day, with the cats shut in their garden house so they couldn't get in the way, I did. Not without event. I put the first place down in the main part of the room, pivoting the Welsh dresser, the sofa and the heavy carved bureau over it as I worked – and then discovered I'd got the rolls of carpet mixed. The second piece was actually the larger. Fortunately I hadn't cut any of it to fit. I rolled up the first piece, heaving the furniture back over it as I went, had a snack lunch and worked on. It was late afternoon before the room was covered to my satisfaction, and I sat back on my heels to survey the result. White walls, oak beams, deep-piled carpet and the old carved furniture back in place – it looked, as it was, a spacious, comfortable room with two and a half centuries of occupation behind it, needing only one thing to complete the picture – a roaring log fire with two cats in their Snoozabed in front of it, which was what, in next to no time, I had.

Worn out with the day's efforts, I trundled off to bed accompanied by my furry henchmen, woke around three in the morning and couldn't go back to sleep, and came down to have another look at my handiwork. Saph came with me. I made some tea and we sat there sharing Marie biscuits.

'Looks good, doesn't it?' I said to Saph, gazing round the room. WOW, he agreed enthusiastically. Any more Biscuits? he enquired, standing up against my knee to check for himself. At which moment, suddenly, from upstairs, there came a clarion call. Tani was addressing us from the landing. What were we Doing down there? Didn't we know the Time? We ought to be in Bed, she bawled. Obviously she had no intention of joining us. Like a Victorian parent she lectured us sanctimoniously from above and I found myself actually feeling guilty.

'We're coming,' I shouted defensively, gathering up my cup and saucer. Hurry Up, bawled her ladyship. 'We're coming,' I yelled again. Anyone hearing me would have thought that I was mad. Anyone seeing me would have been sure of it. So harassed was I by Tani's harangue that in a moment of nervous stress I found myself putting the teapot in the refrigerator instead of emptying it.

Next day it was Saphra's turn to upset our rural tranquillity. Looking again at the newly decorated sitting-room I decided that the one thing needed to complete its appearance of cosy winter country living would be one of my grandmother's honey-coloured brocade draught curtains over the door. I had a pair of them in the chest on the landing. I brought one down, spent an hour taking up the hem to fit the low-lintelled door, inserted the hooks in the runner bar and stood back to admire the effect. Pretty good, I thought, stooping to recover one of the bobbles that had fallen off the curtain edging. The curtain was, after all, very old. I threw the bobble for Saph to chase and he raced after it with delight, tossing it in the air and batting it round the room till eventually he lost it. He came back and sat by the door looking at me expectantly. With apologies to my grandmother, but I could never resist that intent little face, I pulled another bobble off the curtain and threw it for him. The worst thing I could have done, because Saph was no fool. By that time he'd realised where they were coming from.

When he'd lost that one – at least, I presumed that he'd lost it – he came back and sat down again, and when I pretended that I didn't know what he wanted, he took another bobble off the curtain with his teeth. I laughed, and said how clever he was. Off he went, and in no time was back for another. He was on his hind legs now, reaching up to his limit to get it... at which moment the telephone rang. Immobilised, I chatted to the caller, one worried eye on the curtain on which the bobbles were now missing to above Saphra's reach. As I watched, he shinned up the curtain, climbing like a monkey, pulled off a bobble, came down with it in his mouth, and dissappeared with it round the corner.

Suspicion began to dawn. He couldn't be losing them at *that* rate. Excusing myself to my caller I rang off hurriedly, rushed round the corner after him and was just in time to see what he was doing. Eating them. With evident relish. Bobbles that were, I calculated rapidly, a good fifty years old or more. Washed, but nethertheless probably containing residue dust of half a century. I dreaded to think what that could be doing to his stomach.

With more apologies to my grandmother – feeling guilty about it, but she loved cats too, I reminded her – I fetched the scissors, cut off the remaining bobbles (it seemed sacrilege to throw them away so I put them in the bureau drawer) and rang Lanford to ask what I should do. They'd probably go through him like everything else he'd eaten, they told me. Just watch him carefully to see what happened and ring them again if I was worried. Off my own bat I gave him some sardines in oil to lubricate the bobbles – it was helpful in cases of blockage, so I'd read – and every time I passed the bureau during the course of the evening a black-faced cat leapt ahead of me on the to the top of it, breathing sardines heavily on the cottage air and waiting for me to lift the lid so he could help himself to some more bobbles. Some cats never did learn.

In due course the ones he'd swallowed passed safely on their way. Another Siamese crisis was over. It was no good, though. It just wasn't my week. On Saturday Bill the ambulance man appeared, accompanied by a helper in the shape of a youth called Norm – tall, lanky and decidedly gormless-looking, he reminded me of Rodney in 'Only Fools and Horses'. And in their inimitable, unbelievable way they started digging a passageway behind the cottage.

It had been dug out previously, years before, but more earth and stones had since slipped down the hillside and piled up against the back wall. It was making the kitchen wall damp, and in places the pile-up reached to quite a height. It needed clearing out and cementing, said Bill. It would be a tight squeeze, working in that narrow space, but he and Norm would do it in two shakes of a turkey's tail. Where would I like the rubble dumped?

The earth and small stones could be spread over the lane, I told him. It would help build up the surface. But the larger stones had better be put in the long grass on the verges, behind the part I kept cut. I didn't want them damaging my neighbours' car axles.

So they delved and dug and loaded the debris into a wheelbarrow, which Norm trundled out into the lane, putting the large stones where I directed and spreading the rest over the lane surface under my supervision. When I decided he could be left to get on by himself I came indoors to do something else. An hour or so later I made them a cup of tea, and while they were drinking it I wandered out into the lane to look and nearly had a fit.

Piles of rubble dotted the surface like molehills, obviously tipped straight out of the wheelbarrow and left. Each one had its quota of rocks and large stones sticking out of it like bumps on a landmine. All it needed was Poppy Richards to come down from her cottage in her car, or Miss Wellington to prospect past in the other direction, for the fat to be really in the fire.

Why hadn't he spread the stuff out as I'd asked him? I demanded of the hapless Norm. He'd dumped so many stones on the verges there weren't no more room – they kept rollin' down, he said. And Bill was shovellin' so fast he din't have time to level out the loads before he had to run back with the wheelbarrow. 'Keeps I goin' till I nearly meets meself comin' back,' he assured me. 'An' Bill said the cars 'ould level it out.'

So there was nothing for it but to get out there with a rake, scramble the rubble about as best I could, and heave the big stones on to the verges further up the lane. Thank goodness I got it done before Miss Wellington came past on surveillance bent and said how nice it was of me to be improving Poppy's surface for her.

We did our best, I panted weakly. After which Bill and Norm departed, informing me that they'd be back on Monday to do the cementing – Bill had Monday off and Norm, it seemed, was temporarily jobless – and I went indoors and lay on the floor to try to unwind my back with Tani and Saphra sitting pointedly beside me asking me what on earth I was doing lying about like that. Didn't I know it was time for their Tea?

THIRTEEN

The only real snag on Monday was that Bill arrived at 8 a.m. with the cement mixer he'd hired from the DIY and Norm, who must have been brighter than he looked, didn't turn up till nine, whizzing down independently on his motor-bike. This meant my having to help Bill unload the mixer from the home-made camper in which he'd brought it – the camper having been converted by Bill from a secondhand ambulance. The cement mixer got caught on a bed-fitting inside the van; we had a job to unhook it and it was a hazardous job lowering it to the ground; but by the time Norm arrived saying sorry he was late but he had to do an errand for his mum, it was in situ in the yard with Bill busy churning up the first brew of cement in it and I was able to retire and feel my back for signs of breakage while the two of them got on with laying the path round the rear of the cottage, watched by Tani and Saphra from the cat-house window.

They were there so they couldn't get on the cement – or into the mixer, which would have been a distinct probability with Saphra. They stayed there until the path was finished and Bill and Norm went home, having got the cement mixer on board the camper without my assistance. Bill gave strict instructions that the path should be left for two days to set hard before anybody walked on it, so I blocked it at either end with chicken wire and made sure the cats didn't go anywhere near it on their way down from the cat-house, and we settled down for the evening.

I settled, that is, glad that the job was over without too much upheaval. The cats, aware that something interesting had been going on behind the cottage and if they got up into the horizontal window that looked out on to the hillside they could peer downwards and see what it was, spent the evening glued to the glass, making chittering comments at intervals as a mouse or some other denizen of the night trekked, I hoped light-footedly, along the new path. Around eleven I lured them up to the bedroom with a few cat-biscuits while I came down to finally lock up. I checked everything and went up again leaving the sitting-room door propped open: that way they could come down to look out of the windows some more if they liked, but I'd made sure they couldn't get out to the kitchen, and that the outer doors were bolted without a cat's being on the wrong side of them, which was still one of Saphra's chief ambitions.

As soon as I re-opened the bedroom door the cats erupted through it like greyhounds out of a starting trap, pelting down to resume their vigil at the window. I got into bed and started to read while I waited for them to come back again. They didn't usually stay down there very long. I had a book called *The Cat Who Ate Danish Modern* by Lilian Jackson Braun, the writer of a series of American whodunnits whose hero is a seal-point Siamese called Koko, who helps his journalist owner solve some extremely baffling murders. In this one the Danish Modern that Koko ate was not, as I'd expected, some kind of pastry he'd taken a fancy to, but a style of furniture whose upholstery he persisted in chewing, not only ruining it in the traditional Siamese manner but thereby providing valuable clues which eventually solved the mystery. He was also in the process of acquiring a female Siamese companion who was to become his accomplice in further adventures.

As if two masked Machiavellis of my own were not enough, I was absorbed in the machinations of this other pair. I read and read. Tani came up and sat upright on the bed waiting for Saphra to join her: she will never settle for the night without him. I read on. Saphra still didn't appear. There must be something riveting outside the downstairs windows, I thought detachedly...

I must have fallen asleep. Suddenly I woke up, still clutching the book. Somebody was hammering on the front door. I looked at the alarm clock. Ten past three in the morning. The bedside lamp was still on. Tani and Saphra were curled up asleep beside me.

Mind working like clockwork... maybe it was would-be intruders, seeing the light and pretending a breakdown to gain an entry: never open the front door to anybody after dark was my motto... I slipped out of bed and through the bedroom door, closing it so that the cats couldn't follow me, crept into the spare room without putting on the light, opened the window and called out 'Yes? Who's there?'

A torch shone upwards on to a peaked cap and checked hatband and a voice replied quietly 'Police.'

They were after somebody! They wanted my assistance! Just as I'd been reading in *The Cat Who Ate Danish Modern*. How could I help them? I enquired, in unruffled control of the situation. They'd known the right one to come to. I hadn't been on the Parish Council for fourteen years for nothing.

'Are you all right?' asked the policeman, still very quietly.

Puzzled, I said 'Yes.'

'Only all your lights are on and all your curtains are pulled back,' he went on. 'Your neighbours noticed it when they drove down the hill a while ago and they were worried and rang us. Are you sure everything's all right inside?'

I leaned out and looked down. The policeman was right. Light was streaming out across the lawn from all three sitting-room windows. Behind me it was shining out through the bedroom window too – naturally, as I'd fallen asleep with the bedside lamp on. To the right, the hall light illuminated the yard and fishpool. Seen from the road down the hill, it must have looked as if a space ship had landed. I had a good idea how it had happened, too, but I kept my counsel for the moment, just in case. 'If you wait a moment, I'll come down and look around,' I told them.

I opened the bedroom door, grabbed my dressing gown, shut the door once more on the cats and crept downstairs. The policeman and his companions, who'd been out in the lane reporting back to base from the squad car presumably in case they needed reinforcements – were now positioned outside the middle sitting-room window. I opened it, the picture of calmness and confidence, and said 'All's well so far. I'll just look round the back of the cottage.'

'You're sure you wouldn't like us to do it?' asked the first policeman.

'No, I'll be all right,' I said. Leaving them no doubt thinking what a courageous female I was, I inspected the kitchen and lobby beyond it, peered up the newly cemented path with a torch... I was certain there'd be nothing there and there wasn't... and back I went to the policeman. 'Everything's all right,' I assured them. 'I fell asleep reading. I've had a heavy day and must have overlooked the other lights. And' – my voice dropped at this: I didn't know how they were going to take it – 'I've got Siamese cats who like to look out of the windows at night and I always pull the curtains back so they can.'

Their faces were a study. I could see it even in the semi-darkness. I bet they'd never heard anything like that before. 'Glad everything's all right, then. Goodnight,' they chorused weakly and retreated to the squad car, no doubt to phone the station again and wonder whether the sergeant would believe it.

The lights were on at the Reasons' cottage down the lane, too. I phoned them, though it was still not four in the morning. They were probably up and wondering,

I thought. And sure enough they were. They'd been to a birthday party, said Janet. Peter had come up with the dog when they got in, and had thrown gravel at my bedroom window, but I hadn't answered so they'd phoned the police in case... I thanked them for doing it, went back to bed, and told the cats it was all their fault and Bill's. Theirs for insisting on looking out of the windows at night and Bill's for making me help unload the cement mixer. My back would never be the same again, I informed the world in general and the bedroom ceiling in particular, and what the police, and now the neighbours, would think...

I stayed awake the rest of the night worrying about it and next day, believe it or not, I did it again. Went to a local seaside town to do some shopping, took a picnic lunch to eat in the car on the front, sat listening to the news on the radio afterwards – and the next thing I knew, there was a policeman tapping at the car window asking if I was all right. He and his mate had noticed me with my head on the steering wheel as they drove past, he said, and they wondered if I felt ill.

Only tired, I told them. I hadn't had much sleep the previous night. I didn't tell them about the cats, but I had no doubt that there were two police stations in Somerset that day where I went down in the records as an Incident. With either O for Odd or P for Peculiar against my name. Not, as it should have been if there were any justice in this world, SC for Siamese Cats. A week or so later, too, I looked out of the cottage window and saw yet another police car pulled up outside. I wondered what I'd done this time – went out to see, and it was a young policeman who said he was new on the beat and wanted to get acquainted with the valley. I've often wondered since if he was really checking whether I was still showing signs of strange behaviour.

My neighbours would probably have assured him that I *was* peculiar. Always had been. Even Poppy Richards, I was sure, thought I was slightly odd. I was going up the hill in the car one morning when I met her driving down the other way. There wasn't room for us to pass each other, so she drew to one side in a gateway and flashed her headlights for me to go on – which I did, only to spot a blackbird in the road ahead of me, pottering about picking up bits.

It made no move to fly away. Other than Miss Wellington's doves, birds don't around here. They know that no-one in the valley would hurt them. There are pheasants in the forest who congregate on the woodshed roof like sparrows, and flutter down around my head like homing pigeons when I go out to give them corn. I couldn't wait, though, as I normally would have done, for the blackbird to move at its leisure. Poppy Richards was waiting to come down. So I hooted – something Charles had always told me to do, faced with a non-moving bird. They didn't like sudden noise, he said, and would straightaway take off like rockets. The blackbird did, twittering angrily at my colossal cheek. Blasted Woman Driver, it was probably saying. Poppy Richards wouldn't have noticed the blackbird, though, not as far away as she was. Only that I hooted loudly, zoomed up the hill and passed her, hand half-raised in acknowledgment but looking straight ahead. I couldn't look at her – I was going round the corner, where there is rock sticking out of the bank, but that presumably didn't occur to her. That evening she appeared on my doorstep, extremely frosty-faced, asking what she'd done wrong. 'Nothing,' I said, explaining that I'd been hooting at a bird, but I felt sure she didn't believe me.

A curt nod and a 'Goodnight then', and she was gone, slamming the gate as she went. It was a pity, because there was something I wanted to ask her. Something which had me extremely curious.

For quite a while I'd noticed a man going past at weekends, wearing a beard and a wide-brimmed hat like a Bohemian artist and his head bent over a book. A most unusual sight because most people came to the valley to enjoy its beauty and he wasn't looking at it at all. Also, the going is rough past the cottage, with pot-holes and ankle-turning stones. If he really was reading poetry or the classics, as he obviously thought anyone who saw him would think, he'd have fallen flat on his face long before. More likely he was doing it for effect, surreptitiously looking down past the book at the ground – but to what end could he be doing something so ridiculous? And going up the side lane to Poppy's cottage – was he calling on her? She'd been a teacher. Was she running some sort of literary circle in the village of which he was an enthusiastic member?

I longed to know, and now she was annoyed with me and I couldn't ask her. Well, things would sort themselves out, I decided. I shut the door and went back to the sitting-room and the log fire and the cats, which combination gave cause for further development.

Charles, it will be remembered by my readers, had gone in for growing cobnuts, mostly eaten by Lancelot, our resident field mouse, but this winter Lancelot hadn't put in an appearance. Either age had caught up with him and he was now playing a mouse-sized harp or he'd found better quarters for the cold weather. Anyway, there was the nut harvest, for once unclaimed, across in the wood. I went over and gathered a big basketful, beating the squirrels by a whisker: they moved in next day with much squirrel-barking to herald their arrival and buried the rest of the crop in the lawn.

I spent about twenty minutes that evening, reading and eating cobnuts, before Saphra decided he ought to try them too. Wanted Some, he wailed, standing against my knee and touching my hand with his paw. 'You wouldn't eat these,' I said, holding a shelled one out to him and expecting him to reject it. He took it, ate it with gusto and immediately demanded more. He, said Tani, sitting by me with her tail wrapped primly round her feet, was Bonkers. Cats weren't monkeys. They didn't eat *nuts*.

He did. Not only that, when I got tired of cracking them for him and instead threw one in its shell for him to chase, he ran after it, carried it back to the hearthrug, cracked it with his teeth, his head held sideways – then dropped the whole thing on the rug, sorted out the kernel from the shell and ate it.

It became quite a party piece with him that winter – all the more so because his audience laughed to see him do it. When Dora and Nita came to lunch one day and afterwards I laid out a line of cobnuts on the rug to show them, thinking Saph would take what he wanted and it would save me giving them to him one by one, he obliged by cracking them along the row one after the other, eating the kernels as he went. 'How did you teach him to do that?' asked Nora, astounded. It was all his own idea, I said.

He and Tani had lots of ideas between them. Sometimes their perspicacity shook me rigid. Was it, I wondered, because I was alone with them so much, and noticed their behaviour more? Or was it – a theory that occurred to me more than once – that cats were becoming more intelligent with each generation, and therefore gradually becoming more dominant?

I was provided with further evidence in support of my hypothesis just before Christmas. I wanted to see an American Civil War serial on ITV called 'North and South'. The first episode ran from 8 to 10 p.m. I was allowed to watch that one in peace. It was when subsequent episodes were shown at 10.30 p.m., after the news, that I became aware of disapproval.

The cats and I normally went to bed around eleven o'clock. When we didn't – when I sat there sometimes till after midnight, taking no notice of their efforts to remind me of the time – boy, did I get the treatment! Saph pacing round the room like a Victorian father, looking at the hall door. Tani informing me from the back of a chair in a cracked soprano that if I wasn't Careful I'd go to the Dogs. The pair of them sitting side by side in front of me trying to hypnotise me into switching off and heading for the duvet-under which, it seemed, Everybody ought to Be by eleven o'clock.

I found myself feeling guilty. Actually apologising. Sitting on the edge of my chair telling them it was nearly over. Several times I gave in and switched off before the end. Who, I asked them sternly, was boss around here? Two supercilious squints supplied the answer. I had made my bed, now I must lie on it. With them under the duvet, of course.

Christmas came. Saph was entranced. He hadn't seen Christmas decorations before. He poked the prickles on the holly, gazed riveted at the glass balls and glittering tinsel (hanging from spruce branches threaded through the big wrought iron ceiling candelabra: I dared not have a Christmas tree with him around). He stared entranced at the swags of cards strung on ribbons round the walls – to stop him scattering them as he'd been doing when I first set them out in the windowsills and on the dresser and bureau. I put things in funny places, didn't I? he said.

I did indeed, but I couldn't hang the parcels on the walls to protect them from him. Those I had to pile on the table, and remember I only have the one large living-room. Remember, too, how interested he was in the boxes in the bedroom cupboards. The parcels, to him, were boxes, and he dealt with them in the same way. Pushed them off the table with his paw, looked over to see if they'd come open when they fell, got down and tackled them with teeth and claws if they hadn't... Tani sitting on the table saying Nothing was Anything to do with her, but intensely interested just the same. One of the parcels contained, not a present, but a new telephone I'd ordered through the post. It arrived marked FRAGILE:

HANDLE WITH CARE. I heard the bump of that one going down from the other side of the closed kitchen door, and rushed in to pick it up. To tell the truth, I'd been in a hurry when I dumped it on the table or I'd never have left it there. It was all right. It was heavily padded and intact, but it took me a time to open it. Saphra was disgusted. He was even more disgusted when he found it was a telephone. Ought to have been something to eat, he said.

Some of the parcels were, which was one reason why he was so interested in them. Addressed personally to him and Tani from people who'd come here during the year, they contained cat biscuits and packets of Cat Treats and Cat Love. Presents of catnip mice, too: he could have opened a shop with those. And one of them contained a catnip adder, coiled in a Camembert box – a present from a woman in Exeter who had heard the story of the adder on the radio and had managed to find a lifelike length of diamond-patterned cotton for the adder's skin.

I keep it now in the bureau. It is too unusual – and startling – to leave lying around. But when Saph first had it he was entranced. He would swagger round the garden with it – me in attendance of course – pretending he was carrying his Trophy. And there, one morning, Miss Wellington came down the lane and saw him. From outside the gate, at a distance, she let out a scream that rocked the valley. 'An adder!' she screeched. 'Quick! He's got an adder!' And, forgetting in her concern that adders aren't around in December, she came rushing to the rescue, slid on one of the loose stones she was always worrying about, and fell flat on her face. I picked her up, helped her into the cottage, and administered brandy – watched by Saphra who'd followed us in and was sitting by her sniffing the air hopefully; a little brandy wouldn't go amiss with *him* after that scream, said his expression. Fortunately Miss Wellington was quite unscathed. She'd been wearing a woollen headscarf and a heavy coat. 'You and those cats put years on me, though,' she protested, giving Saph the lick off her finger he expected.

They put years on me, too. Take what happened on Christmas Day – this time entirely due to Tani. I'd been invited to lunch with Dora and Nita and their friends, as I had been every Christmas since Charles's death. I was also going to call en route on Jonathan and Delia, the neighbours who'd been such a help to me when he died and who now lived some three miles away. If I left at eleven, I decided, I'd have time for a chat with them before pressing on to Dora and Nita and the turkey. So I took the cats out for a good long session in the garden to make up for leaving them, telling them we'd have a cosy evening together.

Saphra, as usual, was the one I shadowed, keeping him in sight at every step. I'd put them in their garden house at ten, I thought – the heater was already on. That would give them another hour outside while I changed, and filled their hot water bottles and litter trays. Tani was nowhere in sight, but I didn't worry about her. It only needed a call when I wanted her.

And then at ten o'clock, when I called Tanny-wanny-wanny, no Tanny-wanny appeared. I went round the garden, looking in all her hunting spots. Rushed into the cottage and searched that – having first pushed Saphra through the door of the cat-run and shut it. I didn't want him vanishing as well. There was no sign of her indoors, however. Not even on her sanctuary chair. I ran out again, stood on the path by the cat-run and blew a mighty blast on Charles's scout whistle, guaranteed to bring her back from any secret lurking-place at the double in the normal way. No slender, ghost-white cat appeared this time. Only a worried black-faced one, coming through the pop-hole to meet me with a look of pathetic loneliness on his face.

Almost immediately the front gate clicked and Miss Wellington materialised – obviously on her way up to Poppy's cottage, gift-wrapped parcel in hand. Had I heard that whistle? she demanded. As detachedly as possible I said I had. Coward that I was I'd long determined I'd never admit to blowing it to bring the cats home. People would be positive I was scatty.

Probably somebody trying to contact somebody else, I suggested – which was true enough when you analysed it. It had nearly ruined her eardrums, said Miss Wellington, looking indignantly around for the culprit. Unable to spot him, she pattered on up the lane. I withdrew surreptitiously through the back gate and hared fruitlessly up the Forestry track, calling Tanny-wanny-wanny at every bush. Back down again, preparing this time to go up the hill to the Rose and Crown and on round the wide, circuitous sweep where I'd searched, back in the summer, for Saph.

As I stood at the bottom of the hill, ready to start out on my trek – Christmas lunch was out of the question now, I told myself: I'd have to ring my friends to cancel it as soon as I got back – another friend, Tina, companion of my riding days before I damaged my back, came by on her horse Barbary, taking him out for exercise before the day's festivities started. I told her about Tani. She'd look out for her, she said. Go the circuitous way I'd been about to embark on. She couldn't bring her back if she found her – Tani would have fainted in coils before anybody got her near a horse – but if she did spot her she'd ring me from the stables. Meanwhile I'd be free to scout in the other direction.

Along the lane, up the track to Poppy's cottage and on to join the circular route, that was. Dejectedly I set out, up the path to the back gate. Passing the cat-run en route, with Saph still sitting forlornly on the paving stones inside. All Alone, he wailed. Nobody to keep him Company. Where was she, his beloved Tani?

I found out almost immediately. What prompted me to step aside from the path and go and peer through the cat-house window I'll never know. I'd looked through it earlier and she wasn't there. She was now, though. Sitting bolt upright in the cat-bed under the heater, as calm and collected as an ivory statue.

It was no good asking her where she'd been. Obviously she hadn't been anywhere. She must have tired quite early of roaming about in the cold, and gone into the cat-house for a warm: I always leave the door open for them as a quick retreat should danger threaten, and Tani often goes in and sits under the heater on her own. But she hadn't done it straight away this time. She wasn't under the heater the first time I'd looked through the window. She must have been deliberately hiding on the floor, and got into the bed while I was chasing round the countryside looking for her. And no doubt encouraged Saphra to do his orphaned act. Relief flooded over me like an avalanche. 'Phew,' I breathed, mopping my brow. Nothing, said Tani as usual, was Anything to do with her. Fooled me, hadn't they, said Saphra, abandoning his orphan act and coming into the cat-house to join us rubbing heavily round my legs. That was their Christmas Surprise for me.

I made it to Jonathan and Delia's, and on to Dora and Nita for lunch. But I was a nervous wreck for the rest of the day. Fooled me they had indeed.

FOURTEEN

Christmas was over and it was time to reply to all the letters I'd received: letters from people bringing me up to date on events in their own lives, from whom I didn't hear all that often. Siamese owners for the most part, whose experiences defied imagination.

There was the woman who had sent Saphra the home-made adder, for instance. She had a Siamese called Bertie, of whom she'd written to me previously, when he'd kept bringing home white mice. Day after day, and she couldn't think where he'd been getting them, until her husband spotted him one day from the bathroom window going into a shed several gardens away, coming out with a mouse in his mouth and bringing it back over several high walls. On investigation it transpired that the man along the road had rescued the mice from a research laboratory and was temporarily keeping them in an aquarium in his garage, with a box over the top for safety, confident that nobody would know. Bertie had ferreted them out, though – the man had wondered why he kept finding the box off the top of the aquarium – and what with feeling guilty about someone knowing he'd kidnapped them, and Bertie's owners feeling guilty because he kept coming in with them, it was a Siamese manufactured mix-up of the first order. The end of the story was cloaked in diplomatic secrecy – I never heard how they sorted it out – but I do know that later she sent me a photograph from her local paper, showing, heads together, a very paternal-looking Bertie with his friend, a live white mouse.

Now Bertie had put his foot in it again. It seemed his owners' daughter had been married the previous autumn. She was a professional dancer with a troupe in Italy, and had married an Italian musician. Prior to the ceremony, which took place in England, Bertie's mistress had gone over to meet the new in-laws, and they'd taken her on a tour of the country during which she'd been particularly impressed by the Leaning Tower of Pisa and had bought an Italian couture suit to wear at the wedding. Back in England, she got down to the preparations. Made the bridesmaids' dresses. The daughter was wearing her mother's wedding dress: that only had to be altered to fit. Did some house redecoration because people were coming to stay. Made the wedding cake. As a compliment to the bridegroom's family and the tour of Italian architecture, not to mention the effect Siamese cats have on one's sanity, she'd made it as a replica of the Tower of Pisa. What with its odd angle and the pillars it couldn't be transported as it was: it had to be assembled by the chef at the hotel where the reception was being held. He'd said it was quite a challenge, she wrote. I could believe it.

Anyway, the night before the wedding, everything was ready. The in-laws had arrived from Italy. The guests who were staying with her and her husband were already there. Her new suit was on its hanger, suspended from the wardrobe door. Bertie wasn't at all pleased about the visitors – he was marching about with his ears flat – but she was allowed to have people staying *sometimes*, she told him. She decided she'd have an early night and relax. Went to the bathroom to clean her teeth. She was only away *minutes*, she wrote, but when she came back, Bertie, to put his protest on record, had sprayed all down the skirt of her suit.

She'd marched round the house calling him an awful name – which couldn't be true, she admitted, because she had his pedigree showing who his parents were. Her daughter had sponged the skirt and dried it with a hair dryer – it hardly showed at all. And of course it wasn't as pungent as it might have been because Bertie was neutered. But she'd stayed awake half the night worrying about it, stood as far back from people at the reception as she could, and goodness knew what they'd thought. She sent me a photograph which showed her doing it. It looked most odd, as if it was the people she was talking to who were ponging. And the cake was leaning madly sideways on the table in the background. She should have had Bertie at the reception, I told her. Wearing a notice saying It Is All My Fault.

From my friend Pat there was the news that her seal-point boy, Luki, was driving her round the bend as usual. His recent crimes included coming home with a large raw beefburger stolen from goodness knew where and being found sitting on top of a kitchen cupboard astride a turkey which was up there because it was too big to go in the refrigerator, trying to get it out of its wrapping. She, said Pat, had washed her hair by way of relaxing her nerves and had afterwards found herself spraying it with liquid starch. Did I ever do things like that? she asked. I told her about the teapot.

From a parson's wife I heard the story of how, in their previous country living, the rectory was near a duck pond. One day her queen went out and returned in due course with an entire brood of ducklings waddling under her stomach – she with her legs spread so as not to tread on them, looking most self-conscious. They must have mislaid their mother and tacked on to her as a substitute. She couldn't think where she'd Got Them, she said – it wasn't Her Fault... Her expression, said the parson's wife, was priceless. Nobody could believe it. Any Siamese owner could, I said.

Another letter was from an American woman who lived in Philadelphia and for years had kept me up to date with the doings of her cat, Daisy. Some months earlier she had written telling me that Daisy had died and she wasn't replacing her. There could never be another Daisy, and besides, she was too old now to take on another. What would become of it if anything happened to her?

Nonsense, I wrote back. There were always cats around whose owners had died or moved away, and if nobody adopted them they would be put down. She should give a home to one of those. I was sure Daisy would have approved, I told her. She consulted her vet, he agreed, and within a week brought her Daisy's successor. Two years old, timid but becoming friendly: it was nice to have a cat around again, she reported. So there I was, imagining this elderly lady consoling herself with the homeless cat she called Miss Kitty – unable to forget Daisy, of course, but it was someone to cherish... And what had I received in my Christmas mail? A letter describing how Miss K. – the most affectionate, intelligent cat, I understood, that it was possible to meet – was now disrupting the Philadelphia communications system by answering the phone when her new mistress was out.

It seemed that friends calling Mrs C. would, after waiting while the bell rang, hear a crash at the other end as the receiver was knocked off the cradle, then the sound of a cat purring into it loudly. Realising what had happened they would hang up – and Mrs C. would return home to find the receiver on the floor. To avoid it being smashed, she said, she had taken to putting the phone on the floor anyway before she went out, and had actually seen the cat sidling up to it and sitting watching it, waiting for it to ring.

In order to amuse her, Mrs C. went on, one day recently she'd taken off the receiver so that Miss K. could hear the dialling tone – which, after a brief interval, changed to a buzz as a warning that the phone was 'open'. After a minute or so the phone would go dead, but could be reconnected by depressing a button on the cradle, when the whole cycle started up again.

Believe it or not, by being shown how to depress the button (she did it to see it pop up again, said Mrs C.) that cat had now learned not to wait for the phone to ring, but to knock the receiver off, listen for the dialling tone and the buzz, and then re-start the cycle by pressing the button.

Mrs C. was proud as a peacock about Miss K.'s cleverness, and wondered whether Saphra could learn to do the same. Not if I could help it, I replied. I was thinking of tying my telephone up with string.

I was soon to learn the depths of mayhem a cat could achieve in England without even trying. Meanwhile there I was answering letters, the cats curled in the Snoozabed at my feet. Every now and then Tani chittered in a dozy, high-pitched soprano with her eyes closed, about the typewriter Disturbing Her Sleep. Immediately Saphra, also without opening his eyes, would echo her in a low-pitched bass. He didn't know what he was complaining about. He only did it to copy her. Saph, bombastic as he was, Head of the House and In Charge of Everything, still liked sleeping with his head on her stomach and her paw protectively across his neck, as if she was his mum. What she did, he did, and keeping me in order was the order of the day.

So January passed, with indoor occupation. I got a lot of letters written. And Poppy Richards and I were friends again. We'd met up at a neighbour's party and I explained again that I hadn't been hooting at her, but at the blackbird. And I asked her about the man in the wide-brimmed hat who walked through the valley reading, and she said she'd been wondering about him too: she'd thought he'd been visiting *me*. It showed how speculation starts up in a village, and now Mrs Binney started some more. Well, more than speculation actually. This was straight from the horse's mouth. She appeared one day at the cottage gate in a state of agitation, her emerald coat buttoned all awry. Shirl was expecting, she told me. She didn't know what she and Bert were going to do.

'But surely...' I began, then stopped myself.

No point in saying but surely that was the natural outcome of Shirl and Bert living together. In Mrs B.'s eyes it evidently wasn't. Shirl and Bert living together a la mode was one thing. A baby in the offing was another. Shirl and Bert should be in their own place, not a caravan, she insisted. Following, I gathered, a quiet, practically anonymous wedding, Shirl should merge into village life as an accepted ostensibly long-wed, mother-to-be. 'You thinkin' of movin' yet?' she enquired.

I wasn't, I told her, as I'd told her before. This was my home and I was staying in it. I felt like asking why she didn't marry Mr Tooting and let Shirl and Bert have her cottage, but I thought I'd better not. I didn't know how matters stood with her and Mr T. Fred Ferry had stopped telling me of late that he'd seen them around together in the local trysting places – though that might have been because of the weather.

Something would turn up for them, I told her, as helpfully as I could. She mustn't worry about it. People looked at things differently nowadays, even in villages. Think how proud she'd be when she was a grandmother.

Obviously undecided about that Mrs B. plodded back up the hill. Would she be back to try her wiles again? I wondered. Why was it my cottage she wanted for the errant couple, anyway? Because it was picturesque, I supposed. And Bert had professed a liking for it. People were always saying they'd like to live here.

While I was still in the garden, putting bread on the bird-tray, Mr Woodrow happened past with his dogs. I hadn't seen him for weeks. 'You've just missed Mrs Binney,' I said by way of conversation. 'She's just this moment gone back up the hill.'

'Have she?' he said. 'Can't stop this mornin'... In a bit of a hurry...' And paddled off up the hill in her wake. I ought to have suggested she married *him*, I thought. That would have left her cottage free for Shirl and Bert. Sharing it with them certainly wasn't on the cards. It would have looked too much like dire necessity.

There was one bright interlude before the next trauma descended. I went to Connie's New Year party. As a naturalist she had a circle of very interesting friends, none of whom I'd met before. Other naturalists: a man who was an authority on otters and owls and actually kept them; a famous woman botanical artist; a man who made nature films for television and had just come back from filming alligators in the Florida swamps... We sat around her long sitting-room talking to each other – at least, they talked: I sat listening to their experiences with avid interest – until I suddenly spotted Ming, who'd been in the bedroom to begin with but had obviously realised he had a captive audience across the hall. He'd come into the room, edged himself around it behind the chairs and, not bothering with the radiator nearest me, which was the one he'd leaned on to impress me when I first met him, had made his way to the long one under the window at the far end of the room. And there, against the one area of radiator between the chairs that was open to view like a stage, leant his Lordship Ming. Bolt upright, sideways on, his cheek pressed pathetically against the white-painted surface.

'Look,' I said, pointing. Even as the heads swivelled, that cat half-closed his eyes – only half-closed them: he wanted to see the effect – and chicken vol-au-vents and prawns were immediately proffered. Connie put the electric fire in the middle of the room and switched it on in resignation, at which he swayed weakly out, almost Too Cold to Stand, we understood, and stretched full-length on the carpet in front of it. Saphra, I had to concede, had nothing on Ming when it came to histrionics. Ming would have made a pretty good Hamlet.

Now it was February and the snowdrops were out under the beech tree on the lawn, and the pussy willows budding yellow up in the forest. Winter wasn't over yet, though. Came the third week of the month and the sky turned leaden grey and it snowed. Heavily, covering the snowdrops and lying deep on the ground, with Saphra venturing valiantly out into it. Making his way, tail raised, up to the covered area beyond the garage, where he could pretend-hunt among the heaps of stones.

He soon got bored, though. No mice were about in that weather. And I got cold watching over him. I would pick him up and carry him back down to the cottage, where Tani sat sensibly in front of the fire. Sitting by the fire all day, however, wasn't for him. He wanted something more engrossing. That was why, when I found him sitting in the sink one morning studying the cold tap, which was dripping slightly, I didn't call a plumber immediately. Anything that kept that cat occupied and out of mischief was welcome, and the drip kept him mesmerised for hours. Leave it for a while, I thought. It was wonderful to know where he was, and that he wasn't raiding cupboards or baiting Tani.

So the tap dripped and, outside, penetrating frost set in. Frost that lasted for a fortnight, so deep that the septic tank outlet froze and the run-off couldn't get away into the ground and, due to the dripping tap, the tank filled up, back-fired up the pipe and overflowed.

Most people's septic tanks overflow round the inspection cover. At the cottage it came up under the sitting-room floor. When, some years earlier, we'd had our downstairs bathroom moved upstairs, the plumber hadn't sealed off the old pipes as thoroughly as he should have done and, when there was a backfire the water rose up through them. It had happened once before, and Charles had sealed the end of the main pipe thoroughly, never dreaming any of the other pipes could be unsealed. When I spotted a large damp patch on the carpet one Sunday night, however, I knew what it was at once. This time, judging by the patch's situation, it was coming up the old washbasin pipe, which had been covered over with tiles.

I'd deal with it tomorrow, I thought, being a bit of a handywoman. Change the tap washer, have the septic tank pumped out, take up the tiles and reseal the pipe... Simple it seemed until next morning, when the stopcock wouldn't turn off the water supply: it, too, needed a new washer. The tap went on dripping. I dared not take off its top, with the stopcock still full on. The local plumber's wife said he was round the bend dealing with people's burst pipes and there wasn't a hope of his coming for days. The septic tank emptying service couldn't come till Tuesday. The Water Company, whom I rang in desperation, said they didn't deal with washers or inside stopcocks, but they could give me another plumber's name from their list.

When I rang it, his widow said he'd died six years previously, she had frozen pipes herself and she'd been waiting for a plumber for a week. At that point I began to get anxious. Particularly when, belatedly putting a bucket under the drip, I found it was filling at the rate of two gallons an hour. 48 gallons a day, not counting what I normally used. No wonder the septic tank was full up! I fitted a length of hose to the tap, running it out to the snow-covered lawn. That would take care of things till I could get a plumber, I thought. No need to bother with buckets.

Not having a proper tap connection, I used the emptying hose from an old single-tub washing machine, leading it over the sink edge to the main hose so that the drips could trickle away easily. I relaxed that evening, watching TV, thinking how clever I'd been – only to go out at nine o'clock and find the kitchen floor flooded. The end of the hose on the lawn had frozen solid, the drips had built up behind, and the pressure had pushed the other end off the washing machine hose, which was hanging over the edge of the sink.

I mopped up the mess and put the bucket back to collect the drips. I didn't go to bed that night. I dozed in an armchair, Tani and Saphra on my lap, the kitchen timer at my elbow timed to go off every hour. When it did, the three of us erupted like Vesuvius, Tani hid under the sofa, and I trudged out to the frozen wastes of the garden to empty the bucket. Life seemed at its lowest ebb.

Not quite, it wasn't. That came next morning, when the tank-emptying people phoned to say their vehicle had broken down with all the work it was doing and they couldn't come till Wednesday. I rang the Water Company again, who said they were sorry, I'd have to get a plumber myself. They could give me a number... I told them about the six-year-old number they'd already given me and they changed their minds. They could send a man to turn off the water at their own outside stopcock till I *could* find a plumber, they offered. Anything, I said, weeping down the mouthpiece with gratitude. I couldn't tote buckets hourly through another night.

Their man came that afternoon, couldn't find their stopcock which was somewhere under the ice outside the garden wall, and while he was searching for it fell in the stream. With his feet wet, he too altered his mind. He changed the kitchen tap washer in minutes – happening to have one with him in the car, he said; said he'd locate the Company's stopcock when the weather was better, and drove off at top speed to dry out. I tottered indoors and gazed at the cause of it all, stretched out peacefully, paws twitching, on the Snoozabed with his head on Tani's stomach. Nobody would ever believe it, I decided.

FIFTEEN

Spring brought the daffodils out in the valley. A vast yellow sheet of them flowing down the opposite hillside, where Charles and I had planted them years before. A sea of the paler wild variety rioting in the field beyond the cottage, where Annabel was buried, and in the Reasons' wood further down the lane. It was called Daffodil Valley even before our time, on account of the wild ones, and people still came to see them and stare over the gate at Saphra, regarding them with his Sherlock Holmes look from the other side.

It was Saphra who solved the riddle of the man in the big hat. Our mysterious visitor was even more in evidence now. At weekends he seemed to be going up and down the lane continually, and it was then that the solution half dropped on me. He must have heard about its being called Daffodil Valley, and he either was an amateur poet or was hoping to be taken for one. I bet the book he was huddled over was Wordsworth, I thought. And sure enough one morning Saph squirmed under the gate, marched up to him, and looked enquiringly up at the hat. The man, bent over his book, saw Saphra at his feet and stooped to pat him, closing the volume abruptly. *The Poems of Wordsworth* I saw in gilt letters on the spine and reported it to Poppy as soon as he'd gone. He was a poet, or that way inclined: not a spy in disguise as Fred Ferry had insisted whenever the question cropped up. What was there to spy on round here? I'd asked on one occasion. 'Durin' the war they used to put decoy lights up on Black Down,' Fred informed me darkly. What that had to do with it I couldn't think, but Fred always was a one for drama.

I started gardening – weeding the borders, cutting the grass. I spent hours up by the cat-house, digging between the herbaceous clumps, while Saphra watched intently from the corner of the run. He knew what I was doing, and every day, when I let them out after I'd finished working, he'd make straight for the border and dig an enormous hole himself. It was easy in the earth I'd just turned over, and Saph didn't believe in unnecessary exertion. Sometimes, when he'd finished, he wetted in the hole. Sometimes he dug it simply for the sake of doing what I did. Tani, whom I have never known to dig a hole in her life (ladies always use Litter Trays, according to her), usually walked straight down the path and into the cottage while this was going on. On one occasion, however, she went deliberately in the other direction; up the path and past him towards the garage. He stopped to watch her, forgot what he was doing, and when she'd gone past left his excavation and started after her. Recollecting himself at the edge of the lawn, he turned back, and was digging the hole deeper – he always believed in going down to his elbows – when she sauntered tantalisingly back past him again. He kept his eyes on her as he dug – and was so traumatised that he actually started moving towards her like a miniature plough, paws scooping out the earth as he went.

Sometimes I wondered whether that cat was in his right mind. He always seemed to dig his holes inordinately deep – but invariably after he'd sat on them, gaze fixed on the distance, busily thinking Higher Thoughts, they'd be filled to the brim like miniature ponds. Sitting on a hole, too – it seemed it had to fit his bottom exactly, and sometimes it didn't, and he had to move away and dig another. He could have written a book on *Digging Holes for Cats*. I reckon it would have rivalled *The Specialist*.

Cat-befuddled as usual, a week or so later I once more went up to London for a Siamese Cat Club meeting. It meant getting up early to drive to Bristol to catch the London train. Getting up even earlier to give the cats their exercise in the garden before I went, otherwise they'd have raked everything out of the bedroom cupboards while I was away. It was six-fifteen in the morning when I opened the door to take them out, and nearly leapt out of my gumboots with surprise. There, milling about in the yard like a crowd in a fairground, was a pheasant cock and ten attendant hens.

The local pheasants had been coming to me for food for years. The cats knew them, and realised they were too big for them to catch. They – Tani and Saph – would walk round the corner of the cottage and up on the path one behind the other, chittering under their breath at any odd pheasant that happened to be on the lawn, but gazing straight ahead pretending not to see it, which would presumably have undermined their superiority.

The thing was, the current dominant cock – after an absence of several weeks during which he was probably occupied in courting displays in some secluded clearing in the forest – had been coming in the past few days with two or three hens, guarding them, standing back and watching over them proprietorially while they ate with the air of having brought them to his own special restaurant, then shepherding them away again over the wall and into the woods. He came back on his own when he wanted a meal himself – presumably it was infra dig to eat with his wives. I had wondered, though, whether two or three hens was the extent of his harem. And now, at six-fifteen in the morning, here was the answer. He had ten of them!

He looked, I thought, rather embarrassed that I had discovered his secret. The hens looked hopeful for a general handout. Tani and Saph, faced with such a mêlée and unable to do their no-seeing act past that lot, dived into them without delay. Hen pheasants went up in all directions, lumbering into the air like jumbo jets, their wide-spread wings frustrating any attempt by the cats to stop them, while the cock stood his ground, flapping his own wings defiantly, his neck stretched tall, bawling raucous defence calls. I waved my arms shouting 'Stop it!' till the yard was cleared, and the cats continued sedately on their way up the path, smug expressions on their faces, Saph stopping to spray the wall at the top of the steps to remind the pheasants Who was Who round here...

Small wonder that I had little time to get myself ready. That in due course I shot off in the car to drive to the station with hastily snatched-up earrings stuffed in my handbag. Small wonder either, when I got to the hotel where the meeting was being held and attempted to make myself presentable, that I discovered I'd brought one gold stud earring and one of those brass-topped, double-pronged paper fasteners; the sort used for putting through holes in piles of papers. I didn't use it as an earring, but I might as well have done. Nobody in that Siamese-benighted audience would have noticed it.

Back to the valley, and within days there was another crisis. It was breeding time for the foxes and a vixen, hunting for food for her cubs, had on two consecutive days taken one of the Reasons' ducks. They disappeared in the late afternoon, a cloud of white feathers on the Reasons' lawn showing what had happened, and until Janet could get someone to put the survivors in early on a regular basis I offered to do it for her. All I had to do was call them if they weren't in sight, she said, rattle the feeding bowl which she'd leave ready filled with corn, and they'd come straight from wherever they were and make for their house.

Maybe that was what they did when she called them – I'd heard the cacophony of goose and duck voices that greeted her when her car went down the lane in the early evening – but when I went out and banged the bowl at three in the afternoon there was dead silence. I banged again. I shouted. 'Coo-coo' was the only thing I could think of, not having had the sense to ask Janet what she called them, but still there was no reply. 'Coo-coo-coo' I bellowed again, which made a change from being heard bawling 'Tanny-wanny-wanny' or 'Saffy-waffy', but I doubt whether it persuaded anybody within hearing distance that I was less than three-quarters round the bend. And then Gerald and his wives came marching in single file down the hill, round the corner and into the pond, making a terrific show of drinking, washing and flapping their wings, and followed seconds later by the three surviving ducks. Which raised a problem, because Janet had said I need only put the ducks in; the geese could take care of themselves till she got home. But the geese were between the ducks and their house, and since Gerald chose that moment to start mating with them all I could do was stand and wait for him to finish.

Most embarrassing it was, a goose underneath, Gerald on top, Gerald falling off, the pair of them rolling about in Rabelaisian abandon in the pond, then Gerald determinedly climbing back on top again. I explained why I was there to a girl going by on her horse, not wanting her to think I was a voyeur. I doubt whether she believed me. I explained again to a woman I'd never seen before who came drifting along picking up sticks and informed me, apropos of nothing, that she was a countrywoman.

I was waiting to put the ducks in because two had been taken by foxes, I said. 'Ah... foxes,' she chirruped brightly. 'Do you ever hear the young foxes calling in the night? I always remember hearing them when I first came to live in the country.' I refrained from saying that what she'd heard was a vixen screaming for a mate, in case she thought I had a one-track mind, but felt bound to contradict her when she started talking about hearing weasels screaming when they were caught by a fox. Foxes didn't catch weasels, I told her. That noise was a weasel killing a rabbit. 'Oh, is it?' said the would-be countrywoman airily.

She went on gathering sticks. I got over the fence and headed for the pond. The geese made off when I waved a branch at them, but the ducks immediately tried to follow them. I was jumping backwards and forwards over the fence like a retriever and had herded two ducks into their shed and was trying to round up the third, which was rushing about like a demented hen, when the woman came drifting back. 'What about trying it with a carrot?' she suggested helpfully. I didn't tell her that ducks don't eat carrots but I was beginning to wonder about the countrywoman business.

It was mating time everywhere just then. A Siamese-breeding friend I hadn't heard from for ages rang to tell me of the trouble she was having with her Golden Burmese male. She'd gone to buy a queen the previous year, she said, but while the breeder was actually making out the pedigree this absolutely gorgeous kitten walked up and looked at her, and she fell for him and bought him instead. She'd heard that the Burmese-Siamese cross was wonderful, and had the idea of using him as a stud with her Siamese queens. The trouble was, he was now a year old and he still didn't know what was expected of him. At first he used to hide when the queens started calling, so she took him to her vet to have him checked. The vet had up-ended him, pronounced that he had the biggest balls he'd ever seen on a cat, and said there was nothing wrong with him. Give him time and he'd work it out, he said.

She was on hand when daylight did start to dawn. One of the queens was calling, rolling on the floor yelling, waving her paws, Claude looking on in mystification – when suddenly the penny dropped. His face cleared. He knew what was wanted. He got down, threw himself on his back, and rolled as well. Waving his paws in the air, bawling and looking backwards over his head at the queen. He did it now whenever the girls came on heat – and that was all he did. He had such a limp paw, too, and she was wondering... Was it because she'd called him Claude?

I was in the middle of laughing when a thought suddenly struck me. Some while before, Pat had told me that Luki had a habit of rolling on his back, waving his paws and peering backwards at her chocolate-point girl, Sahra. Pat described it as Luki trying to look alluring. Sahra, she said, always looked more horrified than allured. I'd told her that Saphra often did the same thing with Tani, and Tani usually slapped him on the nose. Why should our respective boys try to look alluring? I wondered now. Could they possibly be odd like Claude?

I needn't have worried. A few days later we had an incident that proved who was the man about the cottage. It was a hot day, and I'd propped the cat-house window open so that Tani and Saph could sunbathe on the shelf inside. Going past on my way up to the garage I saw Tani sitting on the shelf, for all the world like a mediaeval princess at a tourney, gazing at the knight wearing her favour in the jousting ring below; and down in the jousting ring – the paved run of the cat-house – crouched Saphra, one paw upraised at something hidden behind a clump of grass. I was in there in an instant, grabbing him. Behind the grass, head up and hissing, was an angry adder.

I rushed Saph down to the cottage, tossed him in, shut the door and ran back armed with a spade. There was no need to rescue Tani. She was still sitting in the window, watching calmly with her paws tucked under her, knowing that at that distance she was safe. The adder was still there, head up and watching me, tongue flickering in and out. I dealt with it regretfully but firmly. Adders have now been declared a protected species but they weren't at that time – and how else can one deal with an adder in a cat-run? From its size I reckoned it was the one that escaped Jeanine McMullen and myself the previous year. Probably it had wintered under the cat-house, which is on bricks; grown bigger; had come out to bask in the sun and, in the way of snakes, would have gone on doing it, a constant and predictably fatal danger to the cats, if I hadn't happened past and been suspicious.

It was the final lesson as far as Tani was concerned, at any rate. She is nobody's fool. The next evening I was out on the lawn with the pair of them, dragging a piece of rope around for them to chase. Saph, in his element, was jumping on it wildly, rushing away with his ears flat and coming back to jump on it again. Tani, who had possibly seen the adder come out from under the cat-house and recognised the same sinuous movement in the rope, hardly touched ground as she belted round the corner and into the cottage. It was Saphra's business to deal with snakes, she said. He was the he-cat round here.

Meanwhile, more cats were appearing in the valley. There were new people in the cottage up by the forest gate, Tim and Margaret, and they had a lilac-point girl called Suki. Suki, they said, was shy, and nervous of meeting people, but they used to take her for walks further up the valley, by the stream, and she soon began to explore the neighbourhood on her own. I went round the corner of the cottage one day and saw what I thought was Tani sitting bolt upright on the path outside the cat-house looking down at me, while Saphra was sitting inside looking out at her. 'How on earth did you get out?' I asked in astonishment, making a move to pick her up – and she turned and shot out under the gate and up the bridlepath. She wasn't Ours, bawled Saphra when she had gone – which was now patently obvious. 'Ours' was a pair of pyramid ears and two crossed eyes peering Chad-like over the cat-house windowsill. From the inside, of course.

Tim and Margaret, seeing my two together and thinking Suki was perhaps coming down to sit by their house for company, decided she ought to have a friend of her own and got a seal-point kitten called Cleopatra, who turned out to be of Killdown descent and related to Saphra. I warned them they were in for trouble, and they got it.

It took, as it usually does, a little while for the two cats to accept each other and then I began to get reports about Cleo turning out to be a minx and having an effect on Suki. Suki still went off on expeditions of her own – down to my garden and up to Poppy Richards, where she used to go into the cottage and pretend it was hers and scared Miss Wellington nearly out of her wits one day when she went in and met a large white cat, like a ghost, gliding silently down the stairs. But at home the two of them were playing together. Cleo was stealing Suki's food. More important, Suki – who'd all her life been a Good girl like Tani (maybe it's inherent in lilac queens) – was stealing Cleo's, and belting about the place like a kitten herself. Obviously the experiment was a success.

They both went for walks with Tim and Margaret, Cleo prancing along beside them, Suki, pretending not to be with them, shadowing them far in the rear. The only trouble was, said Margaret – already discovering that, with two Siamese, crises are endemic – that she and Tim couldn't nip up for a drink at the Rose and Crown of an evening any more without a protesting duet through the sitting-room window about People being Cruel and Deserting Them. What she and Tim had to do, she said – she would never have believed it, but I'd been right in my forecast – was to go out ostentatiously, start up the car (parked where the cats couldn't see it), run the engine for a minute or two, then switch it off and creep surreptitiously out and up the hill. The cats, thinking they'd gone off in the car, would then shut up and go to bed. Wouldn't think it possible, would I? she asked. Wouldn't I just, I said.

Adding to the impression that cats were beginning to take over the valley, two new kittens had meanwhile appeared down the lane. The black one with a white star on his chest was called Starsky. His brother, naturally, was Hutch. The Reasons' tabby was now pretty old and given to sleeping a lot, and the kittens had been acquired to look after the place in general and keep the stables free of rats and mice. Hutch, the under-cover kitten, took on that job, and was rarely seen. Starsky, the extrovert, was more of a front man, patrolling the lane, exploring up the hill, and continually coming over the wall to check on my two. He would openly lie under the beech tree on the lawn, calmly studying Saphra, who was threatening him from the cat-house, secure in the knowledge that Saph couldn't get at him. Tani, as usual, was nowhere to be seen. White Slavers, according to her, could come in Disguises.

Starsky also attached himself to the goose and duck patrols. He seemed to have struck up a friendship with Gerald, and I often saw him going up the hill with the gang, or sitting on the hillside with them behind my cottage. Another hanger-on down the lane at the time was a large Muscovy drake called Charlie, who'd flown in one day from a smallholding over the hill, apparently attracted by the ducks. His owners had another, even bigger, drake, which was why Charlie had left home, and they said he could stay here if he wanted. So he, too, got added to what was beginning to look like a menagerie.

No prizes for guessing who was eventually to be seen leading them like the Pied Piper of Hamelin, of course. I'd parked my car outside the front gate one morning, ready to take off for town. I'd put the cats in the cottage, gathered up my coat and handbag, gone out to get in the car – and there, surrounding it, were Gerald and the geese and Charlie and the ducks; Gerald as usual admiring his reflection in the car panels.

'Out of the way,' I said, waving my arms. The crowd shuffled back a fraction. Leaving, in the foreground, a black kitten with a white star on his chest, inquisitively examining the wheel arches. The geese and ducks, I knew from experience, would scatter when I started the engine. Starsky – I wouldn't like to bet on what he'd do. I wasn't taking any chances, either.

Picking him up, I started down the lane to take him home. Gerald and the geese fell in, honking, behind me. Behind them waddled Charlie and the ducks, for all the world like a Scouts' and Guides' parade – until halfway down the lane Charlie, realising where we were going, decided to show the others he knew. He took off and passed us all, quacking, at shoulder height, and flew on down to perch on the terrace wall. A horse, coming up the lane, panicked, turned and bolted, his rider with her arms around his neck. Fred Ferry, appearing, knapsack on back, round the corner, said 'What d'ust think thee'st be doin? Runnin'a circus or somethin'? Thee bist lucky that 'ooman din't come off!' And all I'd done was try to take Starsky home. I sometimes wondered where the justice was in this world.

SIXTEEN

To be fair to Fred, he had his own worries at that time. Like summer itself, things were coming to a head in the village. I hadn't known much of what was going on beyond the valley, being so busy with my own affairs, and I nearly fell flat with astonishment one morning when Miss Wellington came in to tell me that Poppy Richards and Mr Tooting had been married. At the register office in town, but when they came back from Torquay, where they'd gone on honeymoon, they were going to have a blessing in church. And Poppy was going to live in Mr Tooting's bungalow and her cottage would be up for sale.

Miss Wellington was sorry she couldn't tell me before, she assured me, but she'd been sworn to secrecy. They didn't want a fuss. Oh, that was all right, I said. And nearly fell even flatter when, the following day, Father

Adams's wife told me another piece of news... that Mrs Binney's banns had been called in church on Sunday. Not, as I'd half expected, with Will Woodrow – but with Fred Ferry's father, Sam!

Perhaps she'd seen the way the wind was blowing and pre-empted matters. But I don't really think that was it. She'd been at school with Sam. They'd grown up together. This was obviously what his smartening himself up had been in aid of. And she'd make him a good wife, and they'd neither of them be lonely in future, and she was going to move into his cottage and let Bert and Shirl have hers... Everything was right in the village heaven except for Fred Ferry, who was going round with a face as long as his knapsack at the thought of having Mrs B. as his stepmother, after all he'd said about her.

As for me, there is one last event to record before I finish this chronicle. Revolving, of course, around the cats. I was watching over them one Sunday afternoon while they were having one of their free sessions in the garden. Fortunately I wasn't weeding this time. Just standing with them, cat-crook in hand, up by the garage while they decided what to investigate next. I spotted a girl and a young man coming down the hill with an Alsatian. The girl had the Alsatian on a lead.

I watched them approach the drive gate, which is some forty feet from the garage. The cats watched too, at my side: Tani apprehensive – expecting the White Slavers, as always; Saphra interested because he likes meeting people. You never know who might come in.

What came in that afternoon was a Jack Russell terrier, previously unnoticed because of the Alsatian – squirming under the gate, barking ferociously and nearly falling over himself in his haste to get at the cats. I lunged at him with my crook; he dodged me, still barking; and he and the cats vanished down the path to the cottage in a welter of dust and scraping claws.

I pelted after them, waving my crook and yelling, but they were faster than I was and as I passed the front of the cottage I could hear barking inside. Round the corner I shot, through the kitchen and into the sitting-room. There was no sign of Tani. She was obviously on her sanctuary chair under the table. But in one of the wide-silled windows, at bay with his back to the glass, drooling with fear and his eyes round with terror, was Saphra – and on a low chair beneath the sill, barking its head off and trying to get over the chair-back to reach him – only fortunately its legs were too short – was the dog.

I hit it with the crook and it turned and snarled at me. I hit it again and it fled. Out through the kitchen, back round to the lawn where it stood and barked at me defiantly, while the young man, making no attempt to assist, watched me from the other side of the gate.

'How dare you bring that dog down here without a lead,' I blazed. 'It might have killed my cats. Get it out at once!' It wasn't his dog, he excused himself. He was exercising it for somebody else. Could I catch it for him?

Could I! 'Open the gate,' I shouted. He did. I chased the dog out, and he put it on a lead and disappeared. I went back to the cats. Tani had surfaced and was sitting on the hearthrug quite composedly. Interesting, wasn't it?

she asked. Saphra was visibly shaken and still dribbling with fear. That dog nearly Got Him, he said. I knew it had, and the window glass was cracked where Saph must have hit it trying to escape, but I examined them both carefully and they seemed all right. Until the following Wednesday morning when – they were still sleeping with me – I woke to find blood on the duvet cover. And later, blood on the bed valance.

I examined them again. I couldn't find any blood on either of them. It must be internal. And it must be Saph, I thought. Blood, wherever it was coming from, would have shown up on Tani's milk-white coat. I rang Langford, and they told me to bring him over. I had him there in less than ten minutes, explaining why I thought it was him. Either as a result of hitting his head on the glass, or heaven forbid – something internal. That had been the first sign before I lost Saska. But it couldn't possibly be Tani, I explained. Blood would be so visible on her.

The vet on duty examined Saph all over, including internally, which offended him greatly. You didn't Do That to Gentlemen, he said. She couldn't find anything wrong, she told me, but she'd give him a five-day course of antibiotics, in case he had an internal infection. If the bleeding didn't stop, bring him back on Monday and they'd do further tests.

It didn't stop. It wasn't copious, but it was there. Usually in the mornings, on the bed. By Saturday I was certain he'd be back at Langford on Monday, in spite of his taking his antibiotics so stoically. On Sunday, the last day of his tablets, I woke up sick at heart and leaned forward to examine the evidence. Saph yawned, got up and moved away. There was no blood where he'd been lying. Mystified, I leaned forward more closely, looked at Tani, who was lying with one paw extended – and nearly had a fit. There between the toes of that paw was an angry-looking wound, obviously the cause of all the trouble. One of her claws was missing and she'd obviously been worrying the place with her teeth, making it bleed, and later cleaning off all traces so that unless you parted the toes you couldn't see it. Poor old Saph had had his antibiotic course for nothing.

It was Tani I took to Langford on Monday morning. Apologised. Explained the mistake. The vet, sorry though she was for Tani, laughed heartily. Evidently she knew Saphra's reputation. Tani had broken the claw off at the base, said the vet – no doubt in escaping from the dog – and must have since been trying to pull out the rest of it. She dressed the wound and bandaged it. Tani would soon have that off, I said. So she wrapped the whole leg round with sticking plaster, right to the top, till it looked like a policeman's truncheon. She gave her a course of antibiotics too, and said wait till the end of the week. If I could get the plaster off on Sunday, well and good. If not, bring her back to the Monday evening surgery at 5 p.m. and somebody would do it for me.

I could well imagine myself at Langford for the evening surgery. Tani screaming the place down about White Slavers, my having to pull out afterwards on the A38 with her in the car, when all the office workers were streaming home from Bristol. I worried all the week, while Tani clonked round raising her paw determinedly sideways instead of forwards. Come Sunday I got the plaster off easily. Wouldn't you bet? And her paw had healed beautifully inside it. That was because she was a Good Girl, she assured me.

It is funny when you look back on it. Lots of things are funny in retrospect. Like the woman who wrote to tell me of her Siamese coming home with a joint of beef in its mouth, the carving fork still embedded in it. Like Pat telling me of her new seal-point female, Kiri, bought as companion for Luki, who wasn't turning out to be a good girl at all, but kept going up on neighbours' roofs, round their chimney pots, and bringing home everything under the sun. An enormous piece of pork crackling. An outsize sausage. Goodness knew where she got them. Luki was doing his best – he'd come home with another beefburger. But Kiri was definitely outstripping him: her latest trophy, which Pat had thought was the crust of a large loaf of bread and had gone up the garden to take from her, had turned out to be a whole breaded plaice. They'd be forced to move soon, she said.

There was the cat belonging to an Australian girl who came to see me. She'd left it at home with her parents while she was working in Europe, and one day it had got out and made off down the street. Her mother had rushed out and chased after it – and so, said Marie, had her father, who was confined to a wheelchair. He'd gone whizzing down the road too, and they'd caught it between them. Funny when you visualised it, wasn't it? she asked. Funny it was indeed. The longer one keeps cats – particularly Siamese – the battier I think one gets. Excuse me while I put the teapot in the refrigerator. I do it quite often these days.

Sadly, Doreen Tovey died in 2008, aged nearly ninety. She had thousands of fans of all nationalities and was surrounded by good friends and of course her two cats, Rama and Tiah, who were with her almost to the end. Over fifty years since her first book was published, she has delighted generations of owners of Siamese cats.

Have you enjoyed this book? If so, why not write a
review on your favourite website?

Thanks very much for buying this Summersdale book.

www.summersdale.com